The Green Famil

Christine Smith studied biology, human ecology and
environmental psychology, and for some time taught
social studies. Her interest in food and cookery led to her
training as a demonstrator with the Vegetarian Society in
1983. Working with Sarah Brown, she taught and
developed the Society's Cordon Vert Diploma courses. At
the same time she ran cookery courses, taught cookery to
children and started her own vegetarian catering
business.

Christine Smith lives in Suffolk and is the author of
Casseroles and Bakes and *Good Children's Food*.

The Green Family Cookbook

CHRISTINE SMITH

LONDON
VICTOR GOLLANCZ LTD
1991

First published in Great Britain 1991
by Victor Gollancz Ltd
14 Henrietta Street, London WC2E 8QJ

A Gollancz Paperback Original

A catalogue record for this book is
available from the British Library

ISBN 0-575-05045-4

Photoset in Great Britain by
Rowland Phototypesetting Ltd,
Bury St Edmunds, Suffolk
and printed in Finland
by Werner Söderström Oy

CONTENTS

INTRODUCTION

Are you worried about sprays and pesticides on food? What about additives, preservatives and E numbers?

Are you wondering whether it's a good idea to eat unpasteurised cheeses? Should you peel vegetables? Are microwave cookers safe?

Why do you come home from the supermarket with half a dozen new plastic carrier bags after every visit? Do you find yourself filling your dustbin with mounds of throwaway wrapping from food?

Do you want some good recipes for simple, easy to cook, wholesome meals that are good for you and good for the environment?

Then read on!

The most immediate way of making a positive contribution towards a better world is by taking some active decisions about the food that you buy, cook and eat. Eating is something we do every day, and so every day we can make a positive contribution towards a safer, more environmentally secure future. *The Green Family Cookbook* shows you how to go about making your own choices for an ecologically sustainable future.

Green cooking is cooking in harmony with the environment. Recent years have seen us becoming much more conscious of our surroundings, of the world in which we live and our responsibility to the world and life on it. Green cooking means being thoughtful – making choices and decisions about food, about shopping, about cooking and eating which maintain a balance between the needs of people and the resources of the world. It means understanding the direct connections between people and the world, knowing that just as our actions have an impact on the world around us, so the state of the environment has an impact on us both now and for future generations. By adopting this approach, every day your cooking will contribute to a more secure future for you and your children, and their children as well. You will then enjoy the food that you eat in all ways.

HOW TO BE A GREEN COOK: PRINCIPLES AND PRACTICE

- know that you, as cook and consumer, have the ultimate power to decide whether or not to buy, cook and eat certain foods.
- enjoy cooking and eating as an everyday, pleasurable activity.
- choose food that reduces energy requirements, whether by being locally produced, using minimal packaging, or needing low-energy cooking.
- choose organic food where feasible.
- buy food in season whenever possible, thus reducing the energy input of forced out-of-season production.
- look for food that has not been over-processed – food processing is a great consumer of energy, and your home-cooked food is likely to be much more enjoyable and much better for you.
- think about how you store and prepare food; do you need to use plastic food wrapping, tin foil and kitchen towel, all of which make considerable demands on energy and resources?
- consider whether you really need expensive and energy-consuming gadgets in your kitchen.
- plan your cooking to minimise use of energy, cooking several dishes at once whenever possible, and choosing equipment that is energy-efficient.
- work out a shopping strategy so that, as with cooking and eating, it does not become a headache; shopping locally is often a good way to start this, developing a good store cupboard so that you can take advantage of local seasonal produce.
- devise ways of recycling waste from your shopping, cooking and eating.
- understand the basics of food hygiene so as to reduce the risks of food poisoning.

Above all, enjoy the food you cook and eat!

IS IT GREEN TO BE A MEAT-EATER?

In many peasant cultures meat does not play a prominent part in the diet. It is more of a luxury food for special days and festivals. In Britain, meat has become an everyday food which most people can afford to eat in some form if they want to. This has come about because meat is now produced on such a large scale by intensive rearing methods for the mass market. Over 400 million animals are killed in Britain each year for food. In addition, there is a large market in meat products – pies, burgers and sausages, all of which can use cheaper parts of animals to produce an edible result.

Despite the wide availability of relatively cheap meat, many people do not eat it. The Realeat Company's 1988 survey found that in Great Britain there were 1.3 million adult vegetarians and another 2.4 million adults who do not eat red meat. In addition, 1.2 million children were said by their parents to be vegetarian or beginning to avoid red meat.

Why are people vegetarians?

● animals are inefficient producers of protein; it can take anything up to 10lb of grain to produce 1lb of meat. Meat is therefore an expensive form of protein when compared with other forms of protein available in the shops.
● large-scale meat production involves animals being reared under unnatural conditions, often deprived of space, light, freedom of movement and the opportunity for natural behaviour. These conditions often lead to infection, and the animals are routinely dosed with drugs in order to prevent disease spreading through the herd or flock. Therefore meat may well contain residues of drugs, antibiotics and other feed additives – although most of the major supermarket chains do have policies on residues in meat which their suppliers must follow. Animal feeding regimes can lead to other areas of concern for consumers; feeding recycled

animal protein to naturally herbivorous cattle, for example, has been implicated in the growing incidence of BSE.

● the quality and flavour of factory-farmed meat can be very poor, or at best variable.

● meat contains saturated fats. Studies comparing meat-eaters with non-meat-eaters have found that meat-eaters are more likely to have higher blood cholesterol levels and to suffer from coronary heart disease, high blood pressure, obesity and diabetes.

● eating meat, of course, involves the killing of animals. Although some effort is made to kill animals as humanely as possible, it is usually impossible for the consumer to tell how the animal slaughtered to provide the meat being bought has been handled and killed.

● there is no need to eat meat in order to be healthy. A well-balanced vegetarian diet can be healthy, life-sustaining and enjoyable.

So why do people eat meat?

● meat is a traditional source of protein. Its flavour and texture are part of the traditional British diet, and many people have come to enjoy it.

● it can be easy to prepare and cook.

● meat can be produced ecologically, the animals reared relatively naturally and slaughtered relatively humanely.

● some animals which are reared for meat can live on land which would otherwise be agriculturally unproductive.

● animal life also supplies us with other everyday foods like milk, cheese, butter and eggs. Eighty per cent of beef is produced as a by-product of the dairy industry, so unless we completely avoid any animal products in our diet there will always be meat available for people to eat.

BSE – what you can do about it

It is increasingly believed that cows develop bovine spongiform encephalopathy, so-called 'mad cow disease', from eating cattle feed containing protein from sheep infected with scrapie. Whether the disease can ever be passed on to humans who eat the infected animals is debatable, but public health authorities are obviously worried enough that they are exerting strict control over the disposal of animals infected with the disease in order to prevent cross-contamination, and have banned the sale for human consumption of cattle offal that could be affected.

The practice of feeding naturally vegetarian animals with recycled animal protein in order to boost production of meat and milk has clearly backfired, and as a consumer you must decide what you should do about it.

Many butchers are now indicating that at least some of their meat has come from animals fed only on traditional non-animal-based cattle food, so look out for this. Buy your meat only from reputable sources, and if possible choose a supplier of genuinely organic meat.

Organic meat

An increasing number of farmers are now specialising in the production of organic meat. Some sell directly to the public through farm shops and by mail order, others to the large supermarkets. For meat to be classified as organic by the Soil Association, which offers reliable accreditation to organic produce, the animal's rearing, medication, feed and slaughter are all subject to strict controls, and the Association's standards guarantee that the animal has led as natural a life as possible.

Some 'real meat' producers set their own rigorous standards for the care of their animals, which may incorporate and even go beyond those of the Soil Association. Anne Petch at Heal's Farm in Devon specialises in rearing her own rare-breed pigs and also supplies rare-breed lamb and top quality beef from 'a pedigree Devon herd, allowed to develop naturally entirely free from hormone growth promoters'. She goes on to say that 'once you have sampled its succulent flavour, you will never go back to commercially produced beef!'

At present organic meat costs more to produce than factory-farmed meat, so it will be more expensive. In supermarkets, for example, organic beef typically costs 35 per cent more than non-organic beef. If, however, you choose only to eat meat on special occasions rather than every day, you will probably find that the additional cost will not be too significant.

How to find 'healthy' meat

● when buying meat, choose your butcher carefully. A traditional butcher's shop is more likely to sell local organic meat than a supermarket, so find out what your local butcher can offer. Terms like 'organic', 'home-reared' and 'free-range' are appearing with increasing regularity, and sometimes rather too freely. Ask your butcher or supermarket exactly what each description means.

● some large poultry producers rear chickens which are described as 'free-range'. This can mean that the birds, although still fed the same feed as those kept in factory broiler houses, are kept in large sheds, thousands of birds to a shed, with some access to a small area outside. It is not the image of chickens pecking at grain in the farmyard that many people might imagine. Be careful, labelling can be deceptive.

● look for local producers/suppliers of meat. A growing number of small farmers are rearing 'real meat' to sell directly to the public and to supply to local shops. Try contacting these farmers yourself to find out what is available. If they are some distance away they may well provide a bulk mail order service for customers with freezers.

● if you are buying meat from a supermarket, look out for the organic', 'hormone-free' and 'free-range' labels. If you are in doubt about what a description means in practice, ask.

● think about different types of meat. Though there can be dangers from pesticides, wild meat like rabbit or hare is usually much less likely to be contaminated than factory-farmed meat. If you really want to eat meat, wild rabbit or pheasant is a good natural source. And wherever possible, make sure you choose British produce – for instance, English lamb rather than lamb from New Zealand.

Thoughts for the dedicated meat-eater

● think about whether you really need to eat as much meat as you do at present. Buying real meat from outlets where the animals have been properly reared and slaughtered might be more expensive, but if you ate less of it you would be spending no more on meat and helping yourself and the land.

● would you consider becoming a part-time vegetarian? Many people are already without realising it.

● try to stop thinking of 'meat and two veg' as the basis for a 'real' meal. Vegetarian cookery can be very creative, and as it is often so simple and straightforward you can usually vary a meal by cooking several small dishes rather than one main dish.

● although it still involves the killing of animal life, consider fresh fish as a healthy alternative to meat (see the Fish section, page 131).

Above all, think about the issues and make your own choice!

Suppliers of traditional meat, fish and fish products
Heal Farm, Kings Nympton, Umberleigh, Devon EX37 9TB. Tel: 07695 2077/4341.
The Pure Meat Company, 1 The Square, Moretonhampstead, Devon. Tel: 0647 40944.
The Real Meat Company Ltd, East Hill Farm, Heytesbury, Warminster, Wiltshire BA12 0HR. Tel: 0985 40436/40060.
Ashdown Smokers, Skellerah Farm, Corney, nr Bootle, Cumberland LA19 5TW. Tel: 0657 8324.
Cley Smoke House, Cley, Holt, Norfolk NR25 7RF. Tel: 0263 740282.
Loch Fyne Oysters Ltd, Clachan Farm, Ardkinglas, Cairndow, Argyll PA26 8BH. Tel: 04996 264/217.
River Farm Smokery, Great Wilbraham Road, Bottisham, nr Newmarket, Cambridgeshire CB1 5JU. Tel: 0223 811382/812319.

What about Fish?

As a nation our consumption of fresh fish has declined in the last forty years, whereas our consumption of frozen fish and frozen fish products has increased. A pity really – fresh fish is easy to cook, nutritious and relatively cheap. However, once you start to turn fresh fish into products like fish fingers, the fish becomes very expensive, and may also be laced with food additives and chemicals.

Fish in a green diet

Most fish is caught in the wild – until it is caught it is free-living and feeding naturally. It has therefore not been intensively reared, fed on unnatural food, or dosed routinely with drugs. This does not, however, apply to farmed fish, which should be avoided for the same reasons that factory-farmed meat should be avoided – these fish may be dosed routinely with drugs, can be fed unnaturally to increase production, and are kept in cages. Some fish farming is causing environmental concern as pollution can be caused by the food and drugs used in the production process, some of which stay in the water and are not taken in by the fish. In addition the water can be polluted with high levels of fish excreta.

Fish is highly nutritious – a good source of vitamins and minerals. Fish oils from fatty fish like mackerel and herrings are thought to be particularly beneficial to health. Fish is a low-fat source of protein, and is very easy to cook at home.

Britain is an island surrounded by sea. Unfortunately, exploitation of this natural habitat is possible, and over-fishing, indiscriminate trawling, and even more invasive methods of fishing like the dynamiting that has taken place in the Mediterranean, can result in depletion of this excellent source of natural food.

Bearing all this in mind, it is sensible to include fresh fish in your diet. It is a natural food caught from a natural, often local, environment. It should certainly be chosen in preference to intensively reared, factory-farmed meat.

Dairy Concerns

The British public has become very concerned about the dairy industry in recent years – and rightly so. Hormones, antibiotics and other additives in milk; listeria in soft cheeses; the way animals are reared to produce milk and its products – these are all issues that most people will have heard about.

The modern dairy industry may not seem to show us much of a green approach. The modern milk cow – the Friesian or Holstein – can seem more of a milk machine than a cow, bred as it is for its milk producing capacity and often only with a life-span of three or four lactations.

What about milk as a food?

Milk has often been promoted as the 'perfect' food, being a combination of protein, fats, minerals like calcium, and vitamins. Unfortunately, cows' milk, while being a perfect food for baby calves, is not necessarily the perfect food for humans, whether babies or adults.

Many traditional societies drink little or no milk – our motto of 'a pinta a day' would be thought of as rather unusual in many other parts of the world. Cows' milk has in many cases been linked with allergic reactions, particularly when given to sensitive babies and children.

It is now recognised that colicky babies may simply be showing their intolerance of cows' milk, and even breast-fed babies can be intolerant to traces of cows' milk that pass through to them in their mother's milk. These babies can become much calmer if their mothers refrain from eating any cows' milk products while breast feeding.

Societies which consume little or no milk have a much lower rate of heart disease than we have in the West – this may be a reflection of the high saturated fat content of milk. As a result some nutritionists now recommend that daily consumption of milk should be reduced to a third of a pint a day.

Bovine somatotropin (BST)

The controversial hormone BST has been used experimentally on cows in some herds to increase milk yields without the public being told which herds have been treated. Injections of genetically engineered BST make the cows produce up to 25 per cent more milk than they would normally. While there is little evidence of the dangers of BST to humans – it is in fact a protein occurring naturally in cows – environmental campaigners question the morality and justification for tampering with cattle and the milk supply in this way. In the long run BST may well not be used commercially as there is concern about possible health risks to cows treated with it. In addition, demand for milk has declined and farmers are now faced with stiff milk-production quotas introduced by the European Commission. Britain is not happy to grant the drug a licence and the European Commission has yet to decide whether use of the drug will be allowed. Even if it is harmless to human health there is a great debate about whether it is in fact at all necessary.

What should you do?

On the plus side, milk is a very good source of calcium, a mineral essential to body health in both young and old. Thus, if you limit your intake of cows' milk, care must be taken to ensure that levels of calcium in the diet are kept up by eating low-fat dairy products, goats' or sheep's milk products, and other calcium-rich foods like green vegetables, potatoes and nuts.

Look out for organic milk, now available in some supermarkets. Demand for organic milk has risen sharply, but it is still more expensive than non-organic. Cutting down your milk intake would offset the extra cost of buying organic milk. If your milk comes to your doorstep, ask your milkman for organic milk and see what the answer is!

Choose low-fat milk – many people find that semi-skimmed milk is the happy medium, neither too fatty nor too watery. This will significantly reduce the amount of saturated fat that you consume through using milk. Do not, however, give low-fat milk to children under five – they need the higher levels of nutrients in full-fat milk.

Try using low-fat alternatives to cream – yoghurt, fromage frais, smetana and buttermilk, taking care not to choose the over-processed cream substitutes which often contain additives and sweeteners. Look for alternatives to cows' milk – goats' milk and sheep's milk are becoming increasingly available, even in super-markets. Milk from these animals is often easier to digest, is a good source of protein, minerals and vitamins, and is likely to be produced in a less intensive way without the routine use of drugs and chemicals. There is a long tradition in this country of the suitability of goats' milk as a human food. Sheep's milk yoghurt is now readily available as a Greek-style yoghurt. Unlike cows' milk, sheep's and goats' milk can be frozen, so buy in bulk if you can.

Pasteurisation

Nearly all the milk in Britain is pasteurised – this means that it is heated up to 72°C for fifteen seconds, to kill off bacteria that could cause brucellosis or tuberculosis. However, it also destroys some of the heat-sensitive vitamin C and B vitamins in the milk.

Green-top unpasteurised milk is available in Britain, but only from very limited outlets – usually the producers themselves. This milk comes from cows in an accredited herd. Some people choose this milk because they believe it to be better for you, more natural, and because they know where the milk has come from.

During the listeria/salmonella scares the Government announced plans to outlaw green-top milk. This was met with uproar – and not only from the producers. In June 1989 these plans were dropped and consumers' freedom of choice protected.

The problem of listeria

Government health warnings on cheese? Surely this is difficult to imagine – putting cheese in the same league as tobacco. Yet Government advice is that vulnerable people – the elderly, preg-nant women, young children and those with suppressed immune systems – should not eat soft ripened cheeses like Brie and Camembert. Why?

Listeria is a naturally occurring bacteria which is harmful to human health if, through contamination and poor hygiene, it develops to dangerous levels in foods. It has been blamed for food poisoning, and has been implicated in the birth of babies damaged in the womb by being infected through their mothers eating foods high in listeria while pregnant. Listeria has been isolated in foods like soft cheeses, pâtés and cook-chill foods from supermarkets.

As part of the response to the growing awareness of the problem of listeria the Government did suggest a ban on cheeses made with unpasteurised milk. This suggestion met with strong objection and has not since been put into operation. Pasteurisation kills off some of the bugs in milk but this does not mean that if cheese is made from pasteurised milk the risk of listeria is removed. Well-documented cases of listeria have been traced to pasteurised cheeses, and listeria has been shown to survive pasteurisation.

Perhaps the cheese experts themselves should be listened to. Shirley Webster-Jones of the Oulton Broad Cheese Shop in Lowestoft sells 300 cheeses from around the world, many of which she collects herself from visits to farms and producers. Eighty per cent of her cheeses are unpasteurised. She says, 'If they ban unpasteurised cheeses it would be the end of real food, since these are the real cheeses with real flavour and texture. Raw, unpasteurised milk contains bacteria essential to a natural cheese-making process, and these are destroyed by heat treatment.' She believes that problems with listeria arise from post-production handling and hygiene, and that good cheeses from good producers who know their art is what we should be buying.

What should you do?

Choose your cheese carefully from reputable sources. Do not buy old, stale-looking cheese, and do not buy cheese that is not hygienically or well looked after in the shop. Try cheeses from small producers – the flavour and quality can far surpass the commercial cheeses from large factories – and look out for cheeses made from organic milk, goats' milk and sheep's milk.

If you are in one of the vulnerable groups listed above then be aware of the risk of listeria in some foods, and choose what you eat accordingly.

COOKING WITH EGGS

Eggs have received much bad publicity in the recent past – thank goodness. At the very least the bad news about salmonella in eggs has made us aware of some of the facts about the egg industry and battery chickens. Salmonella in factory-produced eggs has come about partly because of the practice (now finally discontinued) of feeding recycled chicken remains to chickens, and partly because of the inherent problems in rearing animals in factory farms like the battery system.

Free-range

Buy free-range eggs in preference to battery eggs – if your local shop does not stock them, ask until they do. They are now widely available – in shops, supermarkets, and directly from producers. Do not confuse free-range with farm-fresh eggs – this usually means factory-farm fresh! Look for the symbol of the Free-Range Egg Association on the egg-box, although not all producers use this symbol. Free-range eggs come from chickens which have not been reared under the stressful conditions of the battery house, making them less prone to infection, and it is far more likely that they have been fed on suitable, safe food.

Technically, the term 'free-range' means that the hens are able to wander freely in the open, with a maximum 1,000 hens per hectare, although ideally the hens should have more space than this. 'Semi-intensive' means that the hens are able to be outside, but the number allowed is 4,000 per hectare. 'Strawyard' means that the hens are kept inside and only allowed outside access to a straw-covered yard. 'Deep litter' means that the hens are kept inside in large numbers on a floor covered with straw, sand, turf or wood shavings to a maximum of seven birds per square metre, while 'barn eggs' come from hens that are kept inside in very large numbers using a system of perches – obviously this is not the same as the hens being caged as in the battery system, but it is still undesirable.

Whenever possible choose free-range eggs – they will probably be more expensive since at the moment battery chickens are more efficient egg producers, but your choice will be better for you and better for the hens.

Storing eggs

At the height of the salmonella scare the Department of Health advised that eggs should be stored in the fridge. It is now realised that this is not necessary, and could in fact be harmful. Why?

If eggs are contaminated, the bacteria will have already multiplied rapidly well before you get the eggs home, and refrigerating them will not prevent you from being affected. If your egg is infected with salmonella, the only way to protect yourself is to cook it properly. If you cook an egg straight from the fridge it starts off colder, and you may therefore not cook it long enough to reach the required temperature.

So store your eggs at room temperature and cook them thoroughly before serving – some experts say that thoroughly means when the yolk is hard, but if you are sure of your egg supply then you may be happy to eat your eggs when the yolk is still soft.

Suppliers of traditional dairy produce
The Cheese Shop, 74 Beccles Road, Oulton, Lowestoft, Suffolk. Tel: 0502 564664.
The Association of Unpasteurised Milk Producers and Consumers, Path Hill Farm Cottage, Goring Heath, Reading, Berkshire RG8 7RE. Tel: 0734 842365.
The Free-Range Egg Association, 37 Tanza Road, London NW3 2UA. Tel: 071 435 2596.

YOUR KITCHEN

The kitchen can be the focal point of much family life – every member of the family will enjoy spending time in the kitchen, especially if it has enough space for people to do more than basic 'kitchen work'. A cosy, comfortable kitchen can be for eating, reading, chatting, washing clothes and playing in. If you have very small children at home, life is easier if your kitchen is large enough to allow the children to occupy themselves nearby while you get on with your work.

Kitchen design is important for anyone wanting to develop a green approach to food and cooking. A green kitchen is one where, as far as possible, materials have been carefully chosen to conserve the world's resources, while still providing you with an efficient, workable area which is pleasant and comfortable to be in. This means choosing furniture that recycles materials, avoiding materials that might be harmful to you or that denude the environment of valuable resources, and using equipment that is energy-efficient.

Many people, especially those who live in relatively new houses, tend to inherit 'model kitchens', smallish rooms fitted with cupboards, equipment and surfaces which are difficult to move and adapt. While a well-designed fitted kitchen can help us to make optimal use of a small space, most do not. In general, fitted kitchens are expensive to install and cannot be changed without a lot of expense. They are usually made from new materials which include chipboard (containing formaldehyde, which is released into the air and is unpleasant for a person with allergies or sensitive skin), and new timber, often hardwoods from tropical rainforests which are not actively managed and replanted.

The alternative to the fitted kitchen is – not surprisingly – the 'unfitted' kitchen, a kitchen which uses old furniture: cupboards, dressers and tables. There are in fact many combinations of 'fitted' and 'unfitted', and you will probably choose to strike a balance between the two. A more 'loosely fitted' kitchen will help you to reduce the health risks associated with laminates and solvents, can incorporate recycled materials, and will almost certainly be cheaper than a fitted kitchen. It will be more individual, with a ready-made 'lived-in' feel that solid wooden kitchen furniture provides, and you can add 'new' pieces of furniture as and when you can, and change things round if something better comes along. A simple old-fashioned sideboard costing a few pounds from an auction can be brightly painted, and will provide food storage in your kitchen until the perfect dresser or cupboard appears. Of course, in a house with a very small kitchen, simple fitted units may be essential as the only practical solution to kitchen storage, food preparation and cooking. Old furniture tends to be bulkier and can be difficult to fit in and work with in a limited space. Here it would be a good idea to look for fitted units that do re-use old timber, or perhaps find a local carpenter who could do the job for you. Of course, something to remember with an 'unfitted' kitchen; you can take it with you if you move house!

Kitchen design

When thinking about your kitchen, take full advantage of its existing features. If there is an outside north or east wall, for example, make sure that your food storage area is along this wall to take advantage of the natural coolness. Think about where to put food ingredients in relation to cooking and preparation areas. It can be very frustrating to have to walk across the room every time you want a particular oil, herb or spice. If space isn't too restricted, make sure that your kitchen table is big enough for everything that you might want to do in the kitchen.

Cookers

The cooker is the kingpin of most cookery, and the type of cooker you work with is important. A cooker can also be one of the most expensive domestic appliances if bought new. Many people have distinct personal preferences for either gas or electricity; here are some ecological factors to consider.

Gas is a relatively efficient cooking fuel: it is cheaper, and the heat it produces is instant – water comes to the boil on a gas hob far quicker than on an electric hob. Gas is also a relatively environment-friendly fuel, producing the least carbon dioxide and contributing relatively little to the greenhouse effect. Gas does, however, present a risk to health should there be a leak of carbon monoxide or nitrogen dioxide, and this can cause severe respiratory problems. Adequate ventilation and regular safety checks are important with gas cookers.

Electricity is usually thought of as a 'clean' fuel, perhaps because it is invisible. In use it is indeed a very clean fuel and is virtually non-polluting, but the power stations which produce our electricity are major contributors to acid rain and the greenhouse effect. And bear in mind that electric cookers can be up to three times as expensive to run as gas cookers. Thus in both financial and environmental terms, electricity is considerably more costly than gas.

Modern electric cookers are fast and efficient, although an electric hob cannot rival a gas hob for speed and efficiency, and there is a noticeable waste of heat as an electric hob or oven remains warm for some time after switching off the power source. Some people swear by range-type cookers, and an Aga or Rayburn can easily become more a way of life than simply a cooker.

Ranges work on the principle of stored heat, and can be very efficient and economical to use. Different models are available, running on gas, oil, solid fuel, wood or even cheap off-peak electricity. A range will also heat the kitchen, because the actual body of the cooker heats up, and many ranges are connected to hot water tanks which provide all your domestic hot water and even central heating.

Modern ranges are usually very well-designed and insulated, and unless all the stored heat has been used up by a long cooking session, the heat for cooking is always instantly available. A range is expensive, but it will last you a lifetime and rapidly become part of the family.

The only real problems with these cookers result from the fact that while some makes, which are primarily designed as cookers, are excellent at cooking, others have been adapted to run central heating as well and this can make them less efficient as cookers. Find out as much as you can before buying one – personal recommendation from someone who uses this type of cooker daily is the best advice to follow.

Microwave cookers are now to be found in over half the households in Britain. For sheer energy efficiency they take some beating, using very little electricity and apparently cooking food very quickly. However, definite precautions need to be taken if you decide to use one of these cookers. Why?

Microwaves work by agitating water molecules in food, so if there are not enough water molecules they cannot work very well. Food containing high amounts of fat may completely fail to cook through because the fat acts as a blanket preventing the water molecules from heating up. The actual microwaves only penetrate some two inches into relatively solid foods, and cooking the centre depends on the heat being conducted inwards.

Microwaves have been clearly shown to fail to cook some types of food evenly and safely. If you use them for certain foods, therefore, you run a risk of food poisoning from bacteria like salmonella, campylobacter and listeria. This is particularly serious if you use microwaves to reheat ready-prepared dishes or cook-chill meals, or to cook foods already containing bacteria like salmonella-infected chicken. The inner portions of the dish may become only lukewarm, providing an ideal breeding ground for food poisoning bacteria.

The Consumers' Association suggests that it is unsafe to use a microwave to reheat any cook-chill or ready-prepared dish, particularly if you are in one of the high risk groups – the elderly, the very young, pregnant women and people with suppressed immune systems either as a result of illness or drugs.

If you already own a microwave and want to continue to use it safely, there are some guidelines that you should follow:

● do not use it to reheat ready-prepared meals when it might put sensitive people at risk.
● increase the cooking times stated in recipes.
● mix up food during cooking if possible so that the inner portions move nearer to the outside and the penetrating microwaves.
● allow food to 'stand' after cooking as stated in the instructions; this is to allow the necessary conduction of heat inwards.

● plastic clingfilm can be used to cover food while it is being microwaved, but it should not actually touch the food. The plasticisers in some clingfilms can pass to the food, especially fatty food, although recent scientific opinion has ruled out the health risk to humans.

There are more sophisticated types of oven available which combine microwave cooking with conventional heat cooking. The two different types of cooking can be used separately, simultaneously or in combination depending on the model of cooker. If used sensibly this type of cooker can give you the energy savings and speed of microwaves with the safety and thorough cooking of conventional heat cooking. These cookers also can be used to overcome the other disadvantage of cooking with microwaves which is the inability of the microwave to brown and crisp food. Another point to bear in mind, however, with any of these superfast cookers is that they may encourage the use of more ready-prepared meals, which then means you will be eating more processed foods and will therefore also be throwing away more packaging.

Fridges and freezers

Fridges and freezers are important pieces of equipment in a modern kitchen, particularly if you use convenience foods or wish to keep food fresh at home for some time. When buying ready-prepared chilled food or frozen food it is most important that you do not break the 'cold chain' set up by the manufacturers by storing it at too warm a temperature. If the cold chain is broken then you may be exposing yourself to the risk of food poisoning (see page 30).

Fridges and freezers usually run on electricity, but the efficiency of different models varies considerably. Some use twice as much electricity as others to keep the same amount of food chilled or frozen. Until electrical goods are routinely labelled with this type of consumer information you will need to rely on organisations like the Consumers' Association which have tested various makes and models and reported on their relative efficiency.

The Consumers' Association found that at 1989 prices the

quarterly cost of running a fridge varied from £2 to £5, and the quarterly cost of running a fridge-freezer varied from £4.20 to £10 depending on the efficiency of the model. The Association goes on to say, 'Fridges consume electricity at a slow rate compared with other domestic appliances, but because they're plugged in twenty-four hours a day, the energy used mounts up ... Clearly, having an efficient fridge won't save you much money, but conserving energy is good news for the environment as well as for your pocket.'

Refrigeration is a particular environmental concern because of the continued widespread use of CFCs in the refrigerant and insulation of fridges and freezers. CFCs are released into the atmosphere every time a fridge or freezer is scrapped and broken up, and CFCs are now widely recognised to be a major cause of damage to the ozone layer which shields us from harmful ultra-violet radiation in the atmosphere.

CFCs used in the refrigerants of old fridges can be recycled – check with your local council to see if they will recycle your old fridge for you. Ozone-friendly coolants are being developed for use in fridges and freezers, so if you are buying new, look out for CFC-free equipment. Try and sell your old model rather than scrapping it.

Cooking pots and pans

The type of pots and pans you use affects your cooking in many ways. Thin, cheap pans can make hard work of even simple cooking, as everything will stick and burn, and although economical to buy they may cost you more in the long run as you have to replace either them or the food that you cook in them more often.

The type of pan that you use also has an effect on your energy consumption when cooking. If all your cooking were to be done over an open fire, wood, coal or gas, then the heat would easily be able to reach all of the base of the pan, including all the dents. However, when cooking on the solid hobs of electric cookers and ranges it is very important for your pan to have a smooth, solid base to ensure a good contact with the heat source. Your pans also need to be made of a material that conducts heat effectively so that the food cooks quickly and evenly.

Aluminium pans are among the cheapest pans to buy – if you are going to use them make sure they are the heavier variety with a good solid base. Aluminium pans are efficient conductors of heat, but a thin pan heats up very quickly which can result in burning. Thin pans also dent very easily.

There is currently much debate about the health risks associated with aluminium, and people are often alarmed when they see how cooking an acidic food like rhubarb in an aluminium pan will leave the pan shiny bright and clean. The surface of the pan is dissolved by acidic foods, and the aluminium then passes into the food.

The main link between aluminium and health is its implication in Alzheimer's disease, a form of pre-senile dementia. Experts are unsure, however, whether the problems experienced by some older people are actually caused because their bodies retain and absorb far more of the aluminium in their diet than happens with people who do not develop this disease. Some scientists maintain that most people absorb little of the aluminium in their diet, and a normal diet contains aluminium quite naturally. Aluminium is found in many foods including tea, coffee, cereals and bread. The average daily intake of aluminium is about 6mg, which is well within the safe limits prescribed by the World Health Organisation. Cooking and freezing in tin foil adds a negligible amount of aluminium to the food, but be aware of other concerns associated with tin foil.

Whether there is a serious health risk or not, there is no point in taking in more aluminium than necessary. If you cook in aluminium pans, avoid using them for acidic foods like tomatoes, apples and rhubarb.

The Consumers' Association found that 100g of rhubarb absorbed 4mg of aluminium when cooked in an aluminium pan. When sugar was added, it was found to halve the amount of aluminium absorbed by the food.

Or you could use aluminium pans which are coated on the inside.

Cast-iron pans are heavy, tough and long-lasting. They conduct heat well, retain it extremely well, are energy efficient and are generally excellent to cook with. On the other hand, they are relatively expensive, can be brittle, and may break if dropped on a very hard surface.

Cast-iron pans can be prone to rust – many are now coated inside with either matt black or coloured enamel to prevent the formation of rust. They are easy to clean if they are coated inside – even the most stubborn food stains come off after soaking, and they work particularly well at high temperatures.

Stainless steel pans are more expensive than aluminium, are strong and do not dent easily, and are not affected by acids or alkalis in food. They do not conduct heat well or evenly, neither do they retain it well – many steel pans therefore have a heavy solid base made from a 'sandwich' containing a layer of a highly conductive metal like aluminium or copper. Stainless steel pans work best on low and medium heats.

Glass cookware conducts heat poorly but retains heat well, so is ideal for use in the oven – if you are cooking in glass it is often possible to reduce the oven temperature, making obvious energy savings. Glass is totally stable with acid or alkali foods.

Energy-efficient cooking

Whichever type of fuel or type of pan you use, there are some general guidelines which you can follow to ensure that you are cooking with maximum energy efficiency:

● always make sure that your pan has a tight-fitting lid, and use it whenever possible.

● always choose a pan with a large enough base to cover the hob you are using. If your electric ring has a facility for only the centre of it to heat up, then use this for small pans.

● use a pressure cooker whenever possible; these use far less energy than a conventional pan.

● electric grills are wasteful of heat; again, if possible, just heat up half the grill. However, a grill can be used to finish dishes started on top of the cooker, rather than using the oven to brown them.

● if your cooker has a small oven as well as a standard size one, don't forget to use the small one whenever practical.

● always turn down the heat when possible: pans do not need to be constantly boiling over for the food to cook.

● use a minimum amount of water in cooking. Less water to heat up uses less energy as well as reducing the degree to which water-soluble vitamins in your food are lost in the water.

● when using the oven, think whether there is anything else you can cook at the same time. Cook two of the same dish and freeze one.

● if you have an Aga or a similar type of cooker, remember to cook food in the ovens rather than on the top, if feasible, as this is the way to conserve the maximum amount of heat. Many dishes can be started on top of the cooker and then quickly transferred to one of the ovens to finish cooking.

● small pieces of food cook more quickly. For example, if cooking baked potatoes, cook two small ones per person rather than one large one.

● do not overcook food, particularly vegetables. They will taste better, and be better for you.

● choose quick-cooking or no-cooking recipes whenever possible. Stir-frying, for example, is an ideal quick-cooking, low-energy method of cooking.

Other kitchen equipment and gadgets

You can now buy kitchen equipment and gadgetry which will perform nearly every conceivable task for you. But before you buy, stop and ask yourself if you really need them. Which, if any, will repay the cost of buying them in the first place and the energy costs in using them, cleaning them afterwards, and maintaining them? Do not be tempted by glossy advertising or the thought that a particular gadget is essential – it very rarely is.

Many gadgets, like knife sharpeners, blenders and toasters, appear to consume little electricity in use. The Electricity Association says that an average electric toaster will toast sixty slices of bread for one unit of electricity, and one unit of electricity will blend 700 pints of soup in a blender. However, until all the electrical equipment we buy is properly labelled with its energy efficiency rating it is difficult for us to know exactly how much energy each of our gadgets is using. While individual pieces of equipment might not use much energy each time you use them, when added in with all the other electrical equipment you have in your house your energy demands may be higher than you thought, and you may think that perhaps you should try to reduce your demand on the national grid.

When you are considering buying small items of kitchen equipment, think about the energy used to make it as well as its price. Will it really be indispensible, or will it lie unused for much of the time, taking up valuable working space? Is it essential to the food you prepare and cook?

Can you do the job just as easily by hand?

Let's take the chopping of nuts as an example. If you are doing the job by hand, a good sharp cook's knife will work very efficiently, and you can control just how finely you chop the nuts. Admittedly an electric grinder or food processor will do this job for you very quickly, but it is easy to overchop the nuts, ending up with them ground rather than chopped.

Grating, chopping and slicing can easily be done by hand, especially if you are only preparing a small amount of food. A good sharp cook's knife will do all manner of chopping and slicing for you. If you want to be even more efficient but still do the job by hand, buy a mandoline vegetable cutter – sharp blades on a wooden holder down which you draw your vegetables; the slices or pieces come out the other side. An ordinary four-sided grater is best to use for simple grating, or try one of the French hand-operated julienne machines.

If you regularly cook large quantities of food then a machine like a food processor to help with chopping, slicing, grinding and mixing might well be useful. Be sure to choose one that will do most of the jobs you need doing, rather than separate machines for different jobs. But do remember the energy costs in manufacturing the machine in the first place, the energy costs of using it, and the costs of potential repairs or replacement should it go wrong.

Essential kitchen equipment

Good quality traditional implements will do many of the jobs which a food processor or other kitchen machinery would do for you. Among such traditional implements that you should consider for

SAFE FOOD – A GUIDE TO FOOD HYGIENE

Reported cases of food poisoning in this country are on the increase – not only because the incidence is increasing, but also because more cases are diagnosed as we become more aware of the problem. Food poisoning symptoms from bacteria like salmonella, listeria and campylobacter can vary from a mild headache or stomach upset to severe vomiting and diarrhoea, which in some cases can even prove fatal. Of the 120,000 reported cases of salmonella poisoning in Britain in 1988, fifty were fatal.

Many of the ideas and measures recommended in this book will help to reduce your chances of encountering food poisoning, for example by helping you to ensure that the food that you buy is of the best quality. However, even the most perfect example of some food products can expose you to food poisoning if you do not take care when storing and preparing the food. Here are some steps you can take at home to help prevent food poisoning:

• make sure your fridge and freezer are both working properly. The fridge should maintain a temperature of less than 5°C, although some experts suggest the safe temperature is between 0°C and 3°C. The freezer's running temperature should lie between −18°C and −23°C. Install thermometers in both so that you know what the running temperatures are.
• defrost your fridge and freezer regularly if this does not happen automatically – this helps with energy savings as well.
• get chilled and frozen foods home straightaway from the shops. Do not leave them to warm up in your car. If possible use an insulated box or bag to keep them cool. The Consumers' Association

your kitchen are high quality knives and chopping boards.

A high quality cook's knife with an 8-inch blade made from carbon steel can be sharpened to a very fine edge, and to be most efficient will need to be sharpened each time you use it – just three or four strokes on a sharpening stone or other knife sharpener is enough. This type of knife can be used for many everyday jobs in the kitchen – buy the best quality you can afford. Add different sizes has found that these work significantly in slowing down the rise in temperature in these foods once they are out of cold storage in the shop. Transfer the food to the fridge or freezer as soon as possible so that you do not break the 'cold chain' set up by the manufacturers.

● defrost all frozen food thoroughly before cooking, following the instructions on the packet. Do not put hot or warm food in the fridge or freezer – cool it down naturally and as quickly as possible beforehand.

● reheat cooked foods thoroughly to at least 70°C – this will mean that the food is too hot to eat immediately. Do not reheat food more than once. Keep uncooked and cooked foods separate. It is a good idea to keep raw meat at the bottom of the fridge to stop it dripping on any cooked food and contaminating it. Cover all food in the fridge or freezer.

● never exceed the sell-by or use-by date on foods – do not be tempted by cheap offers in supermarkets on foods beyond their sell-by date.

● use a separate chopping board for raw foods, particularly meat, and make sure you scrub it thoroughly after every use. Wooden chopping boards can harbour bacteria more readily than the plastic ones, and special care must be taken to keep these as clean as possible.

● wash up implements in very hot water with a good washing-up liquid, preferably one of the environment-friendly brands. Rinse everything in very hot water and leave it to drain dry. Drying-up cloths can also harbour bacteria.

● keep your kitchen as clean as possible, wiping up spills and crumbs regularly. Wipe down surfaces with a solution of chlorine-free bleach. Dishcloths need to be boiled frequently to sterilise them, or alternatively you can use disposable paper cloths made from recycled paper.

of knives as you can afford them.

When it comes to chopping boards, keep separate ones for raw and cooked food (see page 30). Wooden boards are traditional and good to work with, but they do need to be kept scrupulously clean. You also need to check what type of wood any new board you are buying is made from – it should obviously be made from woods that are sustainably managed. Some people find the new plastic boards are easier to clean and do not dull the blades of knives so readily. They can be long lasting but, of course, being plastic are made from non-renewable energy sources.

A potato masher is useful, as is a hand-turned rotary whisk (really just as efficient as an electric whisk, and costs nothing to use once you've bought it). Other items well worth considering include a juice squeezer (again far easier to use than the electric variety, especially for small quantities), a stainless steel four-sided grater, a mouli-grater, a mandoline slicer, a pestle and mortar, a garlic press, a sieve, and a hand-operated food mincer.

KITCHEN RUBBISH

The advent of the wheelie bin on many British doorsteps spelled disaster to the green effort. These enormous bins, which we never thought we'd be able to fill, have now become an accepted part of daily life. We regularly and easily fill them with the 300kgs of rubbish that each of us generates each year.

Most of the household rubbish that we generate is dumped into the ground, into landfill sites which are eventually covered over with earth. This causes severe pollution problems since the buried rubbish emits gases – paper waste being one of the main culprits in the production of methane in buried rubbish. Other toxic substances in the rubbish, like the contents of old batteries, household cleaners, and any number of unpleasant chemicals which are part of our daily lives, seep into the soil and pollute the surrounding earth and the water supply. Much of the rubbish disintegrates very slowly – plastic rubbish remains intact indefinitely under the ground; tin cans take many years to break down in the soil. Added to this is the fact that the infilling of such sites is destroying natural habitats and using up valuable land space.

Wheelie bins are an ecological disaster because their size encourages us to dump everything in them that we no longer want. The way in which our rubbish is so conveniently disposed of so quickly means that we can be virtually unconscious of the problems caused by the immense mountains of rubbish.

Yet, if handled properly, much of what is mixed up in these mountains of household rubbish could be recycled, saving energy and raw materials. The problem is that it is almost impossible to recycle rubbish from a wheelie bin.

Recycling rubbish from the kitchen

Everything that goes into a kitchen must eventually come out, either as food which we then eat, waste from preparing the food before cooking, leftover cooked food, packaging which arrives with the food when we shop, or discarded or broken kitchen equipment.

Much of this can be recycled – even the food that is eaten is effectively recycled to produce energy, good health and well-being for the consumers.

Preparing food to cook inevitably generates some waste. However, there are ways in which you can reduce this waste. With good quality organic vegetables there will be little or no need to peel them – as valuable nutrients are found in the outer layers you will be reducing the nutritional value the more you peel. With non-organic fruit and vegetables, however, you may feel happier peeling them, despite the nutritional loss, since washing does not necessarily remove all the chemicals on the surface.

With some non-organic produce you often can't win, since even peeling will not remove chemicals which have been absorbed right into the fruit or vegetable.

In general, however, scrubbing root vegetables and rinsing salads and soft fruits is probably the best balance between nutrient loss and health safety.

Peelings from uncooked fruit and vegetables can be used in several ways. They can be put in the compost bin; if you have a garden this is the most obvious way of recycling your organic waste, providing valuable nutrients and humus for your garden soil. But remember, if you throw in potato peelings, you are likely to get potato plants sprouting all over the garden! You can feed peelings to any animals you might keep – finely chop up the peelings or waste from fruits like apples, grapes, plums, or from vegetables like carrots, parsnips, onions, cabbage and other greens and feed them raw to your dog, or cook them up like a soup for chickens if you have them.

Leftover cooked food

Leftover cooked food need rarely be thrown away. Indeed, if you follow the ideas given here for economical cooking you may find yourself regularly cooking more than you need in order to make use of the heat in your oven or to make use of a glut of a particular ingredient. Here are some specific ideas for using leftovers:

- if you cook more rice than you need, allow what is left to cool naturally, cover it and store it in the fridge overnight. The next day fry up the rice with some onions, garlic, spices, cooked potatoes, cooked carrots or peas, add a little liquid if necessary, and you have a simple spiced pilau.

It is important to keep cooked rice very cool and to use it up the next day, as it can become infected with a bacteria, bacillus cereus, which could cause food poisoning. Always make sure when reheating cooked rice to heat it thoroughly to a high temperature.

- there are lots of ways to use up leftover cooked potatoes. Mashed potato can be fried up as potato cakes or bubble and squeak. Try using it as a filling for a Spanish-style omelette or as a topping for a bean or lentil mixture to make a vegetarian shepherd's pie. Leftover jacket potatoes are wonderful sliced and fried in olive oil for breakfast!

- if you have some plain pasta left over from a meal, stir in a little olive oil to stop it sticking and store it in the fridge – use it the next day as the basis for a salad with tomatoes, peppers and olives.

- whenever you cook dried beans, cook more than you need – cooking haricot beans, kidney beans or chick peas uses a fair amount of energy as they have to be boiled for some time. The extra cooked beans can then be used next day for a salad, mashed with oil, garlic and lemon to make a hummus-type dish, or added to a soup to make it substantial and filling.

- with all leftover cooked food it is very important to make sure that you store it, properly covered, in the fridge and use it within a short time. Make sure that you only reheat it once, and when you do so that you reheat it to 70°C or until it is too hot to eat straight from the oven.

Food packaging

Food packaging makes up a third of the rubbish by weight that we put in our dustbins. In general, this waste consists of plastic, glass, metal and paper, much of which could be recycled. Compared with other countries Britain's record is appalling; at the moment we recycle only 2 per cent of our recyclable household waste.

This is where you as the consumer can make some important choices. You can decide what type of food to buy; you can choose where to buy the food; you can choose to buy food that has been excessively packaged or food that has minimum packaging. Having bought your food in its packaging you can then decide whether to simply throw the packaging away in the dustbin or to find ways of recycling it.

Plastic waste

In this country we have yet to reach the level of plastic waste seen in some other European countries, partly because our consumption of bottled water is still at a relatively low level. If you have been on holiday to Greece you will have seen for yourself the enormous problem caused by the non-returnable plastic water bottles which litter the countryside. Yet unless we alter our packaging policy in Britain we could be approaching the same sort of problem ourselves. And drink bottles are only one aspect of plastic rubbish: stop and look at all the plastic you bring home when you do the shopping – plastic wrapping round cheese, meat, breads and cakes, confectionery of all sorts, fruit and vegetables, ready-prepared foods, frozen foods.

Plastic is derived from oil, but only 4 per cent of our oil is used to manufacture plastics. The Consumers' Association says that plastic can be more energy-efficient to produce and transport than other forms of packaging. The problem with plastic is that it is virtually indestructible in rubbish dumps – it does not break down or disintegrate. There are two possible solutions. Biodegradable plastic, which breaks down slowly in contact with the air, can be used for all items which do not need to be permanent – carrier bags, food containers, plastic food wrapping. This type of production is beginning to happen so look out for plastic labelled as biodegradable. Alternatively it is possible to recycle plastic. However, of the 700,000 tonnes of plastic used each year less than one per cent is recycled, which results in mountains of discarded plastic. The problem of recycling plastic lies in the fact that to do this efficiently the different types of plastic need to be separated when they are thrown away. Germany has introduced deposit schemes on plastic drinks bottles – a similar scheme in this country would go some way to reducing the problem.

Glass waste

Bottle banks are now to be found in most cities and towns, though we still have a long way to go before a bank is within walking distance of every home. However, the recycling of glass is a growing industry: 20 per cent of the six billion glass containers we use each year are recycled, leading to a 25 per cent saving in oil and raw materials used in the manufacture of glass. The drawback of using glass as a packaging material is that it is an energy-intensive product to make, and is heavier and often bulkier than plastic, which is the usual alternative.

Cans

The main materials used in cans are tin, steel and aluminium. We use fourteen billion cans a year in Britain, and at the moment about 10 per cent are recycled through can banks similar to bottle banks. Yet the recycling of cans is a very energy-efficient process – recycling aluminium saves 95 per cent of the energy and raw material costs of manufacturing new aluminium.

Paper and cardboard

Thirty per cent of waste paper and cardboard is now recycled in this country, most of this coming from commercial and industrial sources. Very little domestic waste paper is recycled, but there are now a growing number of paper banks appearing so use them if you have one close by.

What can you do to reduce packaging waste?

● choose loose fruit, vegetables and bread, where possible, rather than pre-packed varieties which are frequently more expensive anyway.
● take your own bags and boxes to the supermarket rather than

coming away with your shopping in the new plastic carrier bags given to you at the checkout. Cardboard is far easier to recycle than plastic and may well be made from recycled pulp anyway. If you do take the carrier bags supplied by the supermarket, make sure you re-use them as much as possible. Some supermarkets give you the choice of paper or plastic bags and most now offer plastic bags which are biodegradable.

● save and re-use plastic margarine and yoghurt tubs. These frequently come with airtight lids, making them ideal to re-use for food storage in the fridge or freezer. Avoid clingfilm or other plastic food wraps. Instead store food in airtight boxes with lids. If you have large quantities of leftovers, use a bowl with a plate over the top or a larger lidded box.

● think carefully about the pros and cons of bottled water, especially when it comes to the packaging. The plastic bottles cannot easily be recycled and are non-returnable. Glass bottles are more easily recyclable, though do remember to take them to the bottle bank! Don't make a special journey by car to the bottle bank – this can defeat the object of the exercise. Take them when you are next going that way anyway. Re-use jars and bottles when you can – for jam making, wine making, food storage, spice and herb jars.

● look out for can collection banks, save your cans and then drop them off next time you are passing – as with glass do not make a special journey. You will often find that very large supermarkets have a selection of recycling banks in their car parks, so use them whenever possible.

● think twice before you use tin foil in the kitchen. Aluminium foil is energy-intensive to produce, so use it sparingly and find alternatives wherever possible. For example, to stop a dish from burning in the oven, place a baking tray on the shelf above and this will deflect the heat in the same way as tin foil. Don't use tin foil for food storage – look at some of the ideas above about how to store food more efficiently.

If you do have to use tin foil, make sure you re-use it as much as possible. Find out from local charities if they collect aluminium foil or ring pulls from drink cans for recycling.

Shopping: What to Buy and Where to Buy It

Green cooking begins with green shopping. The first step in becoming green about your food is to think carefully about what you buy.

Where does our food come from?

Our food economy has developed to such a degree that we import considerable quantities of food in order to extend the seasonal availability of particular foods. For example, outdoor lettuces are grown for sale in Britain's supermarkets in southern Europe, purely to make them available for a longer period. If they were grown here, we would have a much shorter season.

Much of the food in our shops has travelled hundreds and even thousands of miles. Sometimes this is inevitable: bananas and chick peas, for example, simply cannot be grown in this country. I am not suggesting that we should completely cut out of our diet those tasty and nutritious foods from other countries, such as Dolcelatte cheese or Italian tomatoes, but where importing food becomes less acceptable is when the imported goods compete with or replace similar British-grown products on the shop shelves. Why buy imported food if a British-produced equivalent is readily available? Unnecessary food transportation obviously wastes energy and increases environmental pollution.

Apples, for example, are imported from many countries, yet Britain must be *the* apple country of the world – or it certainly used to be. In the book *Orchards*, published by Common Ground, Joan Morgan explains that in the nineteenth century 'the national fruit was the apple, which enthusiasts believed grew better in England than anywhere else in the world'.

Some supermarkets are slowly reintroducing traditional English varieties into their stores, and despite the overriding presence of the French Golden Delicious, you will find boxes of real English apples for sale in many greengrocers, particularly in the autumn.

If a British-produced equivalent is not available, is there something else you could use instead? For example, when English apples are no longer in the shops, what do you put in your child's lunch box instead? Do you choose a Cape Granny Smith, a Chilean Red Delicious or a French Golden Delicious, all of which need large amounts of energy to transport around the world and are often relatively tasteless?

Look for something else instead – an early season carrot or a mild white radish in May or June perhaps; by July you could probably buy a few strawberries or raspberries. Find ways of using local fruits and vegetables to tide you over until late August when the first early English apples like Beauty of Bath come into the shops, to be followed by the unbeatable Cox's Orange Pippin and Russet.

Finding out where food comes from can easily become part of your everyday shopping. The country of origin is usually stated on most packaged food; if it isn't, then ask.

What has happened to food before you buy it?

Unnecessary food processing uses up precious energy and can be very uneconomic; it can also affect the health of the consumer.

Let's start with how the basic ingredients are grown. The use of chemical fertilisers, pesticides and fungicides is part of everyday food production. An apple can be sprayed seventeen times between bud and harvesting, and although things are now improving as farmers become aware of consumers' green concerns, chemicals are still often used indiscriminately, with 'insurance spraying' still far too prevalent.

Chemicals are used to make food grow bigger or more quickly, to make it look better (fungicide waxes sprayed on citrus fruits, for example), to prevent bacterial and fungicidal infections, to kill pests and weeds, and to extend the life of the foods on the shop shelf.

What's wrong with 'chemical' food?

The extensive use of chemicals has, in many instances, led to a build-up of chemicals in and on our food, sometimes even beyond the limits set by the Government.

There is evidence that chemicals which have been banned

because of their health risks are still being used. James Erlichman in *Gluttons for Punishment* describes the results of tests carried out in Britain by the Association of Public Analysts in the early 1980s which showed that samples of lettuces were contaminated with DDT, a pesticide that had been banned years earlier for use on lettuces. And this was not an isolated example – other chemicals like Lindane and Aldrin were also found on foods for which their use was banned.

There is much disagreement about what constitutes a 'safe' dose of chemicals used in agriculture and the food industry. Many symptoms such as headaches, rashes and insomnia, which may be associated with chemical pollution, go undiagnosed, and the links between pollution and health are difficult to prove. However, anyone who has walked through countryside undergoing aerial spraying will readily associate a sore throat or wheezy chest with the cloud that descended from the spray plane.

Environmental health concerns have recently led to several successful campaigns, such as that run by Parents for Safe Food in 1989, which succeeded in getting the pesticide Alar, until then widely used in apple production, withdrawn. Other major concerns include nitrate levels (from fertilisers) in the water supply in areas of intensive agriculture, and the way that animals reared for consumption are fed routinely with antibiotics and other substances which can adversely affect the quality of meat.

Organic food

The concerns outlined above have led to a renewed demand for organic food – food that is produced without the use of chemical fertilisers, pesticides, growth promoters, antibiotics and other unnatural or potentially toxic chemical treatments or additives – in other words food that is produced as naturally as possible. Apart from the considerations of possible damage to human health and the environment through the use of chemicals many people also find that organic foods have a much better flavour and texture than those grown with artificial fertilisers; tomatoes and carrots are sweeter, mushrooms are firmer. Try them yourself and see what you think.

Look in the shops for foods which have been produced organically – ask the shopkeeper or manager. My local greengrocer recently had a box of very fresh-looking leafy spinach in the corner of the shop; only by asking did I discover that it was produced by a local smallholder who eschews the use of chemicals – it was just being sold as ordinary common-or-garden spinach!

In larger shops which sell organic food you could find that the organic product is more expensive than the non-organic equivalent, and that the organic product has been imported, whereas the non-organic equivalent may have been produced in this country.

What do you do?

The two things are inter-related. In this country organic farmers get very little financial help, and there is no incentive for a farmer who wants to make the time- and money-consuming switch to organic farming, whereas there is every incentive to stick with non-organic production. This means that much of the organic food sold in British supermarkets has to be imported. Safeway, for example, estimates that 70 per cent of its organic food is imported. Inevitably this makes the organic food more expensive, although many supermarket chains claim that they do not charge an excessive premium for organic food and try to keep the mark-up as low as possible.

In order to bring the price down we need to buy and demand more organic food from our supermarkets, thereby encouraging production of organic food in this country. And things are changing. Sainsbury's sell 'brown cap' organic mushrooms at the same price as the pure-white non-organic variety, and yet are superior in every way – flavour, texture, size, keeping quality. So look around, and keep asking.

Conservation grade

There are also foods quite widely available which are produced to a 'Conservation Grade' standard. Conservation grade food is produced with the use of a limited range of chemicals which are considered to be safe for the soil, since they break down after use, and safe for the consumer since they are not considered to contaminate the food. The main foods produced to Conservation grade standards are cereals, flours and meat.

Processed food

Our shops today are full of processed foods – chilled, frozen and tinned, snacks, sauces and ready-prepared meals. We are so used to processed foods that we probably do not give it a second thought. Many people now seem to be losing the ability to cook properly; where schoolchildren once learned cookery the lessons are now described as 'home technology', and no longer does this occupy a place in the main curriculum. The science of food now seems more important than the art of cookery with practical cookery classes taking a low priority on the timetable.

The food processing industry is a great consumer of energy and involves the use of large quantities of sugar, salt, additives, colours and preservatives as well as a large amount of packaging that is simply thrown away. Processed food can be very expensive and of poor nutritional value. Potato crisps, for example, are a very fatty and costly way of eating little potato. A *Food Magazine* survey in 1989 showed that fish fingers may contain only 40 per cent fish, and that the fish in them may cost you up to £6 per lb.

A lot of sugar is hidden in processed foods, for example in tinned savouries like baked beans, tomato soup, curries and pasta dishes, fresh and frozen flans and pizzas, as well as in the more obvious foods such as cakes, biscuits, puddings and soft drinks. Why do the manufacturers do this? Sugar is a cheap way of adding flavour and bulk to food, of extending shelf life, of disguising poor-quality ingredients and of pandering to our addiction to sweet things. For example, a commercial cheese and tomato pizza may well contain two teaspoons of sugar, a small tin of tomato soup up to three teaspoons of sugar and tomato ketchup can be 20 per cent sugar by weight. A low-sugar baby rusk can contain more sugar than a doughnut! A small can of cola contains seven teaspoons of sugar and some commercial fruit yoghurts can contain three or four teaspoons of sugar per carton.

Britons are notorious for their high sugar consumption – on average each of us gets through more than 100lb of sugar a year, or a 2lb bag every week.

Many of the health risks associated with sugar are well known. Above all, it is an 'empty' food – it gives you nothing but calories and has no inherent nutritional value. Other foods like complex car-bohydrates from cereals provide us with a much more sustained source of energy whereas sugar is quickly absorbed and used up.

Tips for cutting down on sugar:

● cut out sugar in tea and coffee. Try to avoid artificial sweeteners which are chemical-based and will not benefit you either. Try honey as a pure and healthy alternative.

● cut down the sugar in all your recipes to half the stated amount – most contain far more than is necessary. The recipes in this book contain just enough sugar to make the food sweet. Try some sugar-free recipes.

● look out for low-sugar or sugar-free jams and spreads. Pear and apple spread makes a good substitute for sugar in many cake recipes. Cream it with the margarine, using one tablespoon of pear and apple spread to replace one ounce of sugar.

● cut out fruit squashes, cordials and fizzy drinks, all of which are high in sugar or sugar substitutes.

● make sure any fruit juices you buy are pure and unsweetened.

● make your own fruit-flavoured yoghurts from natural yoghurt mixed with a little fresh fruit or sugar-free jam.

● look for concentrated apple juice which can be used to sweeten very tart fruit like Bramley apples and rhubarb or used to make drinks.

Salt also plays a large part in processed foods. Even cakes, biscuits and bread are sources of considerable quantities of salt. It is used in processing to create a strong flavour and to pad out the flavour of cheap ingredients. Although salt is an essential part of our diet, we tend to eat far too much of it in this country, probably at least ten times too much. This is mainly because our diet is high in processed foods such as bacon, sausages, soups, crisps and ready-prepared meals. Most nutritionists agree that we should cut our consumption of salt from an average of 12g a day to 5g a day.

Tips for cutting down on salt at home:

● do not add salt to vegetables when you cook them. If you need to add a little do it just before you serve them.
● do not put a salt cellar on the table.
● add lemon juice, herbs and spices or natural shoyu (soy sauce) instead of salt in your cooking.
● do not add salt to pastry, cakes and puddings.
● avoid snacks like salted peanuts or crisps.
● try food before adding salt.

Food irradiation

Another development in the world of food processing is food irradiation. Bombarding food with radiation has been found to extend the shelf-life of the food and prevent or delay the growth of certain bacteria. The main criticisms of the process, apart from that of safety, are that it can be used to cover up poor quality food and to keep stale food saleable for longer. The debate about the safety of irradiation continues with arguments from both sides of the fence, there being very little support for it from consumer bodies, who claim that much of the evidence in support of the safety of irradiation has little scientific basis. All of this seems to amount to no more than yet further tampering with our food in the interest of economics. Irradiated food may soon become available in the shops – green cooks would do well to boycott irradiated food as being an unwelcome interference in our food supply.

How can you be green in a world of processed food?

● when you can, buy foods in as near their natural state as possible.
● spend some time in a good wholefood shop (see page 48); wholefood shops generally sell foods that have undergone minimum food processing.
● use whole grain brown rice instead of white rice: apart from tasting better, it contains more B vitamins, iron, calcium and protein than white rice.

- use organic wholemeal flour in your baking and for sauces.
- try and eat something raw every day as part of a meal; a simple salad made from grated carrots, apples and a little yoghurt, for example.
- when cooking a dish like a stew or casserole, cook double quantities and then freeze half – your own convenience food for when you need it.

But remember, *maintain a balance*. In a busy world we are not all going to be able to cook all of our food at home from simple basic ingredients. Some processed foods can play an important part in the life of a busy cook, so choose carefully:

- try to go for those ready-prepared or convenience foods that are free from additives and contain the greatest percentage of natural ingredients.
- remember that some tinned foods can help you create healthy, interesting meals when used in conjunction with fresh ingredients – tinned Italian tomatoes, for example. Tinned chick peas, butter beans and haricot beans are ready-cooked and can also prove invaluable to the busy cook who does not always have time to soak and cook the beans at home – or who has forgotten to do so!
- read labels carefully to see where sugar comes on the list of ingredients. Don't buy it if it is one of the major ingredients.
- look out for tinned foods which are sugar- and salt-free.

The 'monthly' shop

Many people like to shop for all their groceries in bulk. This can be useful, saving on petrol and possibly on time. However, you need to ensure adequate and safe storage for your food – you may need a larger fridge and freezer with higher running costs. By all means shop in bulk if it is economic to do so and you don't find yourself wasting too much, but don't let that exclude looking out for good food in between times at smaller suppliers. Make sure you are able to take advantage of a sudden glut in courgettes on the market, or the excellent herrings that one day appear in your fish shop.

Supermarkets

Shopping in large supermarkets can be useful – some stores have definite green policies about some of the food they sell, and many of the very large supermarkets do have a really excellent range of food. Yet a wide range of choice can often be balanced against the effort needed to wheel the trolley down all those aisles! And if you are pushed for time, remember that it is not necessarily quicker to shop in a supermarket. If you take into account the time it has taken you to get there, find your way around the different aisles and then queue up at the checkout, you may discover that using your local shops would save time after all. If you have driven to the supermarket, don't forget to add in the cost of petrol.

Of course, the great danger with a supermarket is that you will often come out with many items that you had not intended to buy!

Small shops

Small local shops are important to the green shopper for several reasons:

● they can supply you with much of your food without your having to travel long distances.
● they can be much more receptive to customer requests and preference; you can ask much more easily for what you want and complain if it's not available.
● they may well stock local produce from small suppliers, produce which is of very high quality but which would never find its way into a supermarket.
● they are often cheaper than supermarkets, particularly for foods like wholefoods, fish and meat.
● you may find specialist shops which stock foods you would not find in a large, mass-market supermarket.

Here are some examples of the service offered by some of my local small shops. A greengrocer recently was selling fresh wet walnuts from France for 95p per lb alongside fresh wet walnuts from a small orchard just three miles away at 65p per lb. The same greengrocer was also selling boxes of organic Cox's Orange Pippin apples at 18p per lb, again from a local orchard – these apples were deliciously sweet and small, too small to find their way into supermarkets which on the whole demand large glossy fruit of unblemished appearance. Some supermarkets, however, do stock small English apples from time to time, although they are probably not grown locally.

A local baker recently announced that he would bake bread from organic flour for customers to order – he already bakes good wholemeal bread free of all baking additives and flour improvers as a matter of course.

A fishmonger in a nearby market town has herrings at 80p per lb – in the supermarkets they are £1.40 per lb.

The wholefood shop sells walnuts at £1.74 for 500g. In the supermarkets they are £1.15 for 200g, and £2.88 for 500g.

Wholefood and health food shops

Many wholefood shops make a real effort to keep their activities as green as possible. They usually buy in bulk and package foods themselves – often in minimum, biodegradable or recyclable packaging. They usually stock a wide range of good quality flours, grains, cereals, nuts, dried fruits and other natural, unadulterated foods, which are also often organic.

Many wholefood shops sell herbs and spices by loose weight – often providing a wider choice, and much cheaper and fresher, than in a supermarket. They often have good quality but sensible vegetarian convenience foods, excellent for quick meals and in emergencies. You will also find ingredients like natural shoyu (soy sauce) and concentrated apple juice in wholefood shops. These are good substitutes for salt and sugar and bring out the flavours of food well. They may sell organic fruit and vegetables – supplies may be erratic unless they come from nationwide suppliers, but prices will often be competitive. You may also find that they can take advantage of local organic produce, unlike larger shops. Many wholefood shops were among the first to stock environmentally friendly household products such as washing-up liquid, washing powder and cleaners.

Health food shops tend to be more mainstream than wholefood

shops. They still sell flours, grains, cereals and nuts, but these will have been bought in ready-packed, and will therefore generally be more expensive than in a wholefood shop.

Health food shops usually also sell a large range of expensive dietary supplements, vitamin pills, elixirs and so on. If you do not have a wholefood shop nearby, then a health food shop is the place to buy your organic flours, cereals, nuts and dried fruits.

Suppliers of organic produce:
Cereals – Doves Farm, Salisbury Road, Hungerford, Berkshire RG17 0RF. Tel: 0488 84880.

W. Jordan (Cereals) Ltd, Holme Mills, Biggleswade, Bedfordshire SG18 9JX. Tel: 0767 318222.

Pimhill, Lea Hall, Harmer Hill, Shrewsbury, Shropshire SY4 3DY. Tel: 0939 290342.

Rushall Farms, The Manor, Upavon, Pewsey, Wiltshire. Tel: 0980 630264.

Other – Aspall Cyder Vinegar (and Apple Juice), Aspall Hall, Debenham, Suffolk IP14 6PD. Tel: 0728 860510.

Hambleden Herbs, Hambleden, Henley-on-Thames, Oxfordshire RG9 6SX. Tel: 0491 571598.

Suffolk Herbs, Sawyers Farm, Little Cornard, nr Sudbury, Suffolk CO10 0NY. Tel: 0787 227247.

West Country Honey Farms Ltd, Braeside Farm, West Horrington BA5 3EH. Tel: 0749 76483.

Whole Earth Foods, 269 Portobello Road, London W11 1LR. Tel: 071 229 7545.

Street markets

Street markets often offer a wide range of fresh produce at good prices, especially if the market is large or in a city. Market traders tend to use minimum packaging, which may make it more difficult to check where foods have come from, though the stallholder will usually be able to tell you from the labelling on the box where the produce originated. It is also difficult to check on any pesticide residues, whereas the major supermarkets do at least have their own guidelines about acceptable pesticide levels in the produce they sell.

Farm shops

Farm shops are becoming increasingly common, and though they are usually only found in the country you will probably not have to travel far out of a town or city to find them. Here farmers sell their own-grown produce, so you can ask about sprays, pesticides, and other additives. Farm shops often sell good quality own-produced dairy products – milk and cream, cheeses and yoghurt – these may well be organic. Many also sell eggs and honey when available – again you can ask the producer about these and be assured of the quality. A few sell their own 'free-range' organic meat.

Advantages of farm shops are that energy is saved and pollution reduced because produce is not transported to wholesalers and retailers, and they offer very good value because of low overheads and direct selling. They also often help small farmers to stay in business.

Pick-your-own

Pick-your-own is becoming increasingly popular. It gives you the chance to buy fruit and vegetables straight from the field, allowing you to choose the produce that you want. It involves you (and, importantly, your children) in the actual process of food supply, and cuts down on transport costs – so do not travel too far yourself just to pick-your-own!

Picking your own makes it easy to check on sprays and chemicals, and means that you can take advantage of gluts – produce is often sold cheaply at the end of the season.

So each possible shopping place has its own disadvantages and advantages for the green cook. Some choices will be unavailable to you anyway without a lot of travelling, others may not be feasible because you simply do not have the time to visit lots of different shops. What is important is to use the best combination available to you.

Grow-your-own

Growing your own food, however small an amount, is another very positive way that you can make a contribution to the environment by using your own energy and reducing energy requirements in food production and supply, and to your own health. You can also practise organic techniques every step of the way – some companies now supply organic seeds, as well as organic compost and fertilisers.

However, not everybody has room for a vegetable garden. Even if you only have a small paved yard, balcony or windowsill, there are still many things you can grow. Here are a few ideas.

Herbs

Herbs grow well on a sunny windowsill and you may be able to keep them going through the winter. They will also do very well in pots outside in the summer. At the end of the summer pick some to dry. Lie the herbs on paper in a warm, airy place; when dry, crumble and store in a jar in a cool, dark cupboard. Good varieties to choose are:

- parsley: curly and flat-leafed
- basil: Greek basil has a pungent, spicy flavour
- oregano: Greek oregano is especially flavoursome
- mint: spearmint or apple mint are both versatile
- rosemary
- marjoram

Tomatoes

Many varieties are now on the market which are ideal for windowsill and container growing, both inside and out. Look out for sweet cherry tomatoes like Gardener's Delight or Totem. There is even a trailing variety which is designed for a hanging basket. Tomatoes are particularly rewarding to grow; their sweet, juicy flavour is so superior to any commercial tomato you can buy.

Courgettes

Do you have a space outside where you can stand a bucket? Then you can grow a courgette plant and enjoy this well-cropping vegetable fresh for many weeks in the summer. Keep picking the courgettes while they are still small to encourage further fruiting.

Lettuces

Commercial lettuces are usually heavily treated with chemicals and often have little flavour. Growing your own means that you can have freshness and flavour without chemical pollution, as well as trying some more unusual varieties with distinctive flavours. Two good ones to try are Salad Bowl, a non-hearting lettuce ideal for container growing from which you can take just a few leaves at a time while the plant continues to grow, and Tom Thumb, a small cabbage-type lettuce which is also good for a limited space. You can grow your lettuces in a windowbox or other small container outside, or inside on the windowsilll. If grown indoors, lettuces need shading from strong sunlight.

Sprouting seeds and beans

A simple way to start to grow some of your own food is to sprout some seeds to use in salads and stir-frying. Sprouted seeds are a valuable source of vitamins and make a lovely crunchy addition to a meal. Mung beans (from wholefood shops or some large supermarkets) can be very easily sprouted and grow into the bean sprouts so popular in Chinese cooking. Follow this method for foolproof results:

Put a handful of mung beans into the base of a large glass jar. Cover with warm water, leave to stand for two to three hours and then drain off the water. Cover the jar with some muslin or a clean piece of an old tea towel held in place with an elastic band. Stand the jar in a warm spot indoors. If you keep the jar in the dark, the sprouts will be white, if it is kept in the light then the sprouts will become more green. At least twice a day rinse the sprouts with fresh cold water, draining them well before replacing the cover on the jar. This twice-daily rinsing is important as it keeps the growing sprouts fresh, cool and damp. The sprouts will be ready to eat within four to ten days, depending on the temperature and the seeds. Rinse the sprouts well and then keep in the bottom of the fridge until you use them.

Other seeds to try: alfalfa, aduki beans, lentils, fenugreek, mustard and cress. Always make sure that you buy seeds that are meant for sprouting or eating so as to avoid the chemical treatments used routinely on many seeds for garden use.

There are lots of possibilities. Just think about what is practical for you. There is absolutely no reason why vegetables cannot be grown in a flower-bed amongst the roses, or in buckets and tubs outside the door.

Make sure, though, that you do adopt simple organic measures when growing your own vegetables. Whatever you manage to grow will be your own contribution to your food, it will be directly under your control – and you can enjoy the fruits of your labour!

Recommended reading:
Vegetables from Small Gardens – Joy Larkcom, Faber and Faber, 1976, 1986
The Indoor Kitchen Garden – Joy O. I. Spoczynska, Bloomsbury, 1988

Contact:
Henry Doubleday Research Association (HDRA), National Centre for Organic Gardening, Ryton-on-Dunsmore, Coventry CV8 3LG. Tel: 0203 303517.

THE GREEN STORE CUPBOARD

A well-stocked store cupboard is essential for the green cook. Having the basic ingredients to hand gives you the freedom to take advantage of fresh seasonal ingredients when you are out shopping, or fruit and vegetables from your garden, or excess crops given by gardening friends.

Your store cupboard should include:

Dry ingredients

Many of these are best bought from wholefood shops that specialise in selling unrefined foods using minimum processing and packaging and which are also often organic (see pages 48–9). You may find locally produced flours, but most of the products will be imported, since we are not able to grow them in this country.

When buying grains, flours and cereals, remember to think about what has happened to the food before you buy it. White flour, rice and pasta has undergone more processing and refining than the wholemeal varieties and will also have lost valuable nutrients as a result.

Flour   Unbleached white and wholemeal, organic.
Rice   Long-grain organic brown rice is the most useful. It is also much easier to cook than white rice.
Pasta   Wholemeal and white varieties – spirals, shells, spaghetti.
Bulgar wheat   For meals and salads in a few minutes.
Other cereals   e.g. porridge oats, organic.
Nuts   Walnuts, hazelnuts, cashew nuts, peanuts – a good source of vegetable protein.
Dried beans and lentils   Including red split lentils, which cook quickly without any soaking.
Dried fruit   Raisins, sultanas, apricots, dates.
Dried herbs   Thyme, mint, oregano, marjoram, basil, rosemary, bay leaves.

Spices   Cinnamon, cumin seeds, coriander seeds, cayenne pepper, paprika, turmeric, good quality curry powders, garam masala, nutmeg, mustard, freshly ground black pepper, salt.
Baking powder.

Ingredients in bottles and jars

Oils   Almost all oils are imported, since Britain produces only rape seed oil. Choose vegetable oil in preference to animal oil, which is a by-product of intensive meat production here and abroad, and which is high in cholesterol. A good quality olive oil is essential. It will be relatively unprocessed, and richer and thicker than the highly processed oils. Choose a cold-pressed extra virgin olive oil from Greece or Italy for the best flavour. Buy it in large cans from wholefood shops for economy. A light, refined sunflower oil is also useful for really high temperature frying.

Vinegars   Organic cider vinegar and wine vinegars for everyday use, sherry wine vinegar for special recipes.

Shoyu   Natural soy sauce, from wholefood shops and very useful for seasoning.

Concentrated apple juice   Available from wholefood shops and used in both sweet and savoury recipes.

Honey   Clear organic honey, locally produced if possible.

Yeast extract   A useful savoury flavouring rich in B vitamins.

Mayonnaise   Unadulterated commercial variety made, preferably, with free-range eggs.

Mustards   Wholegrain and Dijon are the most useful.

Black olives   Greek-style preserved in salt.

Creamed tomatoes or *passata*.

Tomato purée.

Convenience foods

Choose convenience foods that have undergone minimum processing, that contain no artificial additives and as few as possible other, unnecessary additives, such as sugar, and which will help you to make use of fresh ingredients when they are available. These are the most useful:

Tinned tomatoes have a good flavour, often better than the fresh, commercial tomatoes available in Britain. They have many uses and can help you to make interesting meals easily.

Tinned pulses – chick peas, butter beans, cannellini beans, flageolet beans – can save you a great deal of time and energy and are good value.

Dried foods like VegeBangers and VegeBurgers can be really useful for emergencies and are nutritious and healthy.

Dairy products

Cheddar cheese Preferably a good quality vegetarian cheese made without animal rennet, and other locally produced cheese from small producers.

Parmesan cheese A whole piece or ready grated.

Milk Semi-skimmed or skimmed, possibly organic, or goats' milk.

Vegetable margarine A variety that contains no artificial additives and is not highly coloured or salted.

Butter Use fairly sparingly, as butter is high in cholesterol. It is, however, free of artificial additives and is often locally produced.

Yoghurt Make your own if possible (see page 163).

Milk products Buttermilk, smetana, fromage frais, cottage cheese, etc.

Eggs Always free-range! (See page 18.)

In the freezer

Use your freezer wisely and it will help you to be green.

● freeze extra portions of casseroles and stews when you make large quantities.

● freeze fresh vegetables if you have a glut.

● goats' milk freezes well.

● fill your freezer with good-quality bread so that you always have it available.

Vegetables and fruit

Most commercially grown fruit and vegetables are produced with the help of chemicals – through growing, ripening and storage. It is best to avoid these chemicals wherever possible.

● look for organically grown vegetables and fruit, and for locally produced varieties. See page 58 for tips on preparing fruit and vegetables.
● always have a good supply of organic potatoes – the great British standby available throughout the year. If all else fails jacket potatoes make an excellent meal!
● other all-year-round necessities include onions and garlic, both of which store well.

Fish and meat

Fish and meat are not essential for a balanced diet, and are really extras to a green diet. If you want to include them read the advice on buying and preparing, on pages 10–13 and 131.

THE RECIPES

Putting your green ideas into practice continues with the preparation and cooking of the ingredients that you have chosen. The recipes here are to start you off. They are based on the following principles:

- the use of fresh ingredients where possible.
- vegetables and fruit, grains and pulses form the staples; fish and meat are the extras.
- foods used are in as near their natural state as possible, contain no artificial additives and are organic if at all possible.
- energy is conserved where possible (see pages 27–8).
- meals are not tied to the traditional idea of including a main dish – usually meat or fish and two veg. The Small Vegetable Dishes enable you to make combinations of dishes and accompaniments, rather as in an Indian meal, and encourages reliance on healthy and more economical forms of protein, such as pulses.
- the use of sugar is kept to a minimum without taking all the fun out of eating puddings.

If you don't have all the ingredients for a particular recipe it is often possible to improvise and substitute another similar ingredient with excellent results. After all, cooking and eating should be rewarding, relaxing and enjoyable.

Similarly, don't worry if you are unable to obtain organic produce. Make sure that you remove as much of the surface chemical residues as possible by simply washing and scrubbing the produce. You could peel, if you prefer, though you lose some of the valuable nutrients found just under the skin, and the fibre of the skin itself. Another important point to remember with fruit in particular is that it is often treated with fungicide waxes to prevent the deterioration of the skin in storage and to make the fruits look bright and shiny. These must be removed as far as possible before using, and you can do this reasonably well by scrubbing the fruits in warm soapy water. This is particularly important if a recipe includes grated lemon or orange rind. 'Unwaxed' fruit is increasingly becoming available, even if the fruit itself has not been grown organically.

SOUPS

Soup can be served as a complete meal or as a light first course. It is ideal for using gluts of vegetables, as you can make a large quantity and freeze the extra portions to use later. Don't forget that you can save energy by cooking soups in the oven alongside other dishes. The soups in this section are all vegetable-based. Lentils are excellent in soups, adding thickness, flavour and protein with the minimum of extra cooking. For super-fast substantial soups try using red split lentils which can be ready to eat after only 20–30 minutes' cooking.

Cool Cucumber Soup

A chilled summer soup which requires no cooking. Use fresh mint if you have it.

SERVES 4

1 cucumber	1 pint/570ml buttermilk
1 small mild red onion *or* 2 spring onions, very finely chopped	1 tablespoon concentrated apple juice
1 large eating apple, finely chopped	2 tablespoons chopped fresh mint *or* 1 teaspoon dried mint

1   Grate the cucumber coarsely (peel it first if you wish, although this is not necessary). Pour off any liquid from the grated cucumber.

2   Add the onion and apple to the cucumber and then stir in the buttermilk. Add the apple juice and mint, and chill before serving.

Carrot and Parsnip Pottage

This thick, golden winter soup uses a few simple ingredients, and proves that you don't need a fancy meat or vegetable stock to create really good flavours. The addition of a few split red lentils gives the soup body and thickness as well as protein.

SERVES 4

2 tablespoons olive oil
1 onion, finely chopped
2 medium parsnips, chopped
2 medium carrots, chopped
2 medium potatoes, chopped
4oz/110g split red lentils
1½ pints/900ml water
2 bay leaves

1 teaspoon dried mint
1 teaspoon dried marjoram
1 teaspoon dried thyme
1 tablespoon tomato purée
¼ teaspoon yeast extract
salt and freshly ground black
  pepper

1   Heat the oil in a large pan, add the onion, parsnips, carrots and potatoes and fry gently for 5–10 minutes.

2   Add the lentils, water, bay leaves, mint, marjoram, thyme, tomato purée and yeast extract. Bring to the boil, cover and then simmer gently for 25–30 minutes until the vegetables are very soft and the soup has thickened. Liquidise or mash with a potato masher if you would like a smoother texture. Season with salt and pepper and serve.

Cauliflower and Stilton Soup

Cauliflower needs quite careful cooking to bring out its flavour. Try this subtle addition of a little Stilton cheese to create an unusual, rich-flavoured soup. If you prefer, use Dolcelatte which is more likely to be made using vegetable rennet, or indeed any other blue cheese which may be more locally produced.

SERVES 4

2oz/50g butter or margarine	2 bay leaves
1 onion, finely chopped	juice of half a lemon
2 cloves garlic, crushed	2oz/50g Stilton or other blue
1 carrot, finely diced	cheese, finely chopped
1 cauliflower, cut into small	freshly ground pepper
florets	a handful of chopped fresh
1½ pints/900ml water	parsley

1   Melt the butter or margarine in a large pan. Add the onion, garlic, carrot and cauliflower, cover and cook gently for 10 minutes.

2   Add the water and bay leaves. Bring to the boil and then simmer again with the pan covered for another 10–15 minutes. Remove from the heat and mash the soup into a purée.

3   Add the lemon juice, pepper to taste, and then the cheese, stir until melted and serve, sprinkled with parsley.

Lentil Soup

This wonderful, nourishing cross between a soup and a stew originates from Greece.

SERVES 4

1lb/450g brown lentils	a large handful of chopped
3–4 tablespoons olive oil	fresh parsley
2 onions, finely chopped	2 bay leaves
4–6 cloves garlic, crushed	salt and freshly ground black
3–4 tablespoons tomato purée	pepper

1   Pick over and wash the lentils. Put in a pan and cover with cold water. Bring to the boil, cover and boil fast for 10 minutes. Simmer gently for a further 20–30 minutes, until the lentils are almost cooked. Drain and set aside.

2   Heat the olive oil in a large pan over a moderate heat. Add the onions and garlic and cook for 10 minutes until well softened and brown. Stir in the lentils and cook for a further 5 minutes. Add the rest of the ingredients, and cover with water. Bring to the boil, cover and then cook gently for 40 minutes, adding enough water to make the soup as thick or thin as you like. To thicken the soup liquidise or mash a small amount and stir into the rest of the soup. Season with salt and pepper and serve.

Fragrant Tomato and Apple Soup

This is an excellent recipe for using up gluts of apples and tomatoes from your garden or the local market. The flavour of the apples enhances the tomatoes and helps to overcome the tartness of tinned tomatoes if you are using these.

SERVES 4

1 large onion, finely chopped
2 teaspoons ground coriander
2 tablespoons olive oil
2–3 sweet eating apples, grated
1lb/450g fresh tomatoes, skinned and finely chopped

or 1 14oz/400g tin tomatoes, finely chopped
1 tablespoon concentrated apple juice
15fl oz/400ml water
salt and freshly ground black pepper

1   In a large pan, fry the onion and coriander in the olive oil for 5–10 minutes.

2   Add the grated apple, chopped tomatoes, apple juice and water. Bring to the boil, cover and simmer gently for 20 minutes. Remove from the heat and mash the soup with a potato masher. If you would like the soup to be creamy add a little milk; if you prefer a light texture add extra water. Season with salt and pepper and serve.

Italian Chestnut Soup

The large amount of garlic in this recipe gives the soup a wonderful richness. Cook slowly in the oven alongside other dishes for maximum energy efficiency.

SERVES 4

2 tablespoons olive oil
2 small onions, roughly
  chopped
6 large cloves garlic, whole
2 large sticks celery, very finely
  chopped
1lb/450g tomatoes, chopped

or 1 14oz/400g tin tomatoes,
  chopped
4oz/110g dried chestnuts
2 tablespoons tomato purée
1 tablespoon dried basil
2 pints/1.1 litre water
freshly ground black pepper

1   Heat the oil in a large flameproof casserole and add the onion, garlic and celery. Cover and cook over a medium heat for 5–8 minutes.

2   Add the tomatoes and cook for a further 5 minutes. Add the chestnuts, tomato purée, basil, water and a little pepper. Bring to the boil, cover and cook in the oven 350°F/180°C/gas mark 4 for about 2 hours, until the chestnuts are soft. Liquidise or mash about half of the soup and return to the pan to make the soup thick and smooth before serving.

Spicy Mushroom Soup

Mushrooms mildly spiced with coriander and cumin make an elegant soup. The flavour of organic mushrooms is far superior to that of ordinary cultivated mushrooms, so look out for them in your supermarket or local greengrocer.

SERVES 4

1oz/25g butter or margarine
1 onion, finely chopped
1 teaspoon ground coriander
    seeds
1 teaspoon ground cumin
    seeds
¼ teaspoon chilli powder
8oz/225g mushrooms, thinly
    sliced
1 tablespoon shoyu

1 pint/570ml water
2 bay leaves
1 teaspoon dried thyme
2 tablespoons bulgar wheat
5fl oz/150ml milk
salt and freshly ground black
    pepper
fresh coriander or parsley,
    finely chopped

1   Melt the butter or margarine in a large pan. Add the onion, ground coriander, cumin and chilli powder, cover and cook over a medium heat for 5 minutes. Add the mushrooms and the shoyu, cover and cook gently for a further 10 minutes.

2   Pour in the water, add the bay leaves, thyme and bulgar wheat, and bring to the boil. Cover and simmer for 25–30 minutes. Remove from the heat and liquidise or sieve some of the soup and return it to the pan to make a smoother soup. Stir in the milk and warm through. Season if necessary with salt and pepper and sprinkle with the coriander or parsley before serving.

Chilled Fennel Soup

The mild aniseed-flavoured fennel makes a refreshing, light soup. If you grow your own fennel in the garden you will find it produces a most beautiful plant.

SERVES 4

1oz/25g butter or margarine	½ pint/275ml water
1 large onion, finely chopped	½ pint/275ml milk
1 clove garlic, crushed	4 tablespoons single cream
1 medium potato	salt and freshly ground black
1 large head fennel	pepper

1   Melt the butter or margarine in a large pan and cook the onion and garlic over a medium heat for 5 minutes.

2   If you would like your soup to be very light in colour, peel the potato; otherwise leave the skin on. Chop into small pieces. To prepare the fennel, chop the head into very small pieces, saving the feathery leaves for garnishing. Add the potato and fennel to the onion, cover and cook for a further 10 minutes.

3   Add the water, bring to the boil, cover and simmer for 15–20 minutes, until the vegetables are well cooked. Remove from the heat and mash the vegetables well, or liquidise if you would like a smooth soup. Stir in the milk, season with salt and pepper and chill in the fridge for several hours.

4   To serve, swirl into each bowl a spoonful of cream and sprinkle with chopped fennel leaves.

Lettuce Soup

Another good late summer soup, useful for when your lettuces are
threatening to go to seed in the garden or for when you manage to
pick up several good ones for the price of one, late in the day at the
market. Serve hot with a swirl of smetana, sour cream or yoghurt,
and crisp garlic bread. It is also excellent served chilled.

SERVES 4

2oz/50g butter
1 large lettuce *or* several small
  heads, chopped
1 large onion, finely chopped
2 cloves garlic, crushed
1 small potato, finely diced

1 teaspoon dried oregano
½ pint/275ml apple juice
½ pint/275ml water
½ pint/275ml milk
salt and freshly ground black
  pepper

1   Melt the butter in a large pan. Add the lettuce, onion and garlic
and cook gently until softened.

2   Add the potato, oregano, apple juice and water. Bring to the
boil, cover the pan and simmer gently for about 20 minutes, until
the potato is cooked.

3   Remove from the heat, liquidise, mash or sieve the soup, add
the milk and warm through. Season to taste and serve.

Gazpacho

Gazpacho is the ultimate no-cook soup; all the ingredients are raw, and it is served cold. But you really do need to use a food processor or liquidiser, though, so some of the energy you save in not cooking you lose by liquidising – a common problem in trying to be green in our world today! This is a delicious concoction, but be warned: the raw peppers, garlic and onion make it unsuited for the delicate digestion.

SERVES 4

1 small cucumber, peeled and
   diced
1lb/450g tomatoes, skinned
   and deseeded or 1
   14oz/400g tin tomatoes
1 onion, chopped
2 cloves garlic, chopped

1 small red pepper, chopped
1 small green pepper, chopped
3oz/75g breadcrumbs, soaked
   in water and squeezed dry
½ pint/275ml water
4 tablespoons olive oil
1 tablespoon red wine vinegar

Garnish

fresh mint leaves
small piece of cucumber, diced

1   Put the cucumber, tomatoes, onion, garlic and peppers into a food processor or liquidiser. Add the squeezed breadcrumbs and ¼ pint/150ml of the water. Liquidise until smooth. Add the rest of the water, the olive oil and vinegar. Liquidise again briefly.

2   Chill and serve garnished with the fresh mint and the extra cucumber.

SALADS

Try to eat some form of salad every day – raw vegetables are an important source of vitamins and minerals, and turning them into interesting salads is easy and energy-efficient.

Green Salad

A good lettuce salad can turn even the simplest meal into something quite special, especially now that so many varieties are available in the shops and as seed. Serve a salad as a separate course, as in France, to really appreciate this abundant salad vegetable. If you grow your own lettuce in the garden or in a tub you could eat this nearly every day during summer, particularly if you choose one of the cut-and-come-again, non-hearting varieties. There are many types of dressing for lettuce; here are just two:

Garlic and Olive Oil

This classic is easy to make in large quantities and will keep for a few days in the fridge in a screw-top jar. The proportions remain the same, however much you make, and you can add as much or as little garlic as you like. For an extra dash of flavour use sherry wine vinegar instead of wine vinegar – you will need only half a measure of sherry wine vinegar as its flavour is much more intense. You can add chopped fresh herbs or dried herbs.

3 measures olive oil
1 measure good wine vinegar
several cloves garlic, crushed

salt and freshly ground black pepper

Mix all the ingredients together in a screw-top jar and shake well.

Smooth Creamy Dressing

Mayonnaise is a versatile ingredient in salad dressings as it forms a good base for different flavours. If you have a good supply of eggs you can make your own; otherwise there are some good varieties available to buy.

6 tablespoons mayonnaise
1 teaspoon Dijon mustard
1 tablespoon olive oil
1½ tablespoons lemon juice

6 tablespoons milk
1 tablespoon tomato purée
freshly ground black pepper

Using a fork or wire whisk mix all the ingredients in a large bowl. Check seasoning and store in a screw-top jar in the fridge.

Potato and Walnut Salad

SERVES 4

1lb/450g potatoes
2 eating apples, chopped
2oz/50g walnuts, chopped
1 small red onion *or* 3 spring
   onions, very finely chopped
2 tablespoons olive oil
2 tablespoons yoghurt

1 teaspoon cider vinegar
1 teaspoon wholegrain
   mustard
salt and freshly ground black
   pepper
2 tablespoons chopped fresh
   mint

1   Boil the potatoes until just tender. Drain, cool and cut into thick slices. Add the apples, walnuts and onion.

2   Mix the olive oil, yoghurt, cider vinegar, mustard and seasoning to taste, to make a smooth sauce. Pour over the potato mixture, mix gently together and serve sprinkled with the mint.

Chinese Coleslaw

Chinese leaf, also called Chinese cabbage, is a crisp and crunchy base for salads. It is a good buy as it keeps well for several days in the fridge. It is possible to find organic Chinese leaf in large supermarkets, and it is also very easy and quick to grow your own at home.

SERVES 4

½ small head Chinese leaf, shredded
1 large red onion or several spring onions, finely chopped
2 sweet eating apples, thinly sliced

3 tablespoons yoghurt
4 tablespoons mayonnaise
1 teaspoon wholegrain mustard
few sprigs of fresh mint (optional)

1   Mix together the Chinese leaf, onion and apples.

2   Combine the yoghurt, mayonnaise and mustard and add a little water if the dressing is very thick. Coat the Chinese leaf mixture with the dressing and serve with the mint sprinkled on top.

Beetroot Salad

This rich, bright salad is very cheering on a winter's day. Make the dressing with walnut oil if you have it – it often comes from small producers in France who use water-based technology to grind the nuts and produce the oil, and if we are going to import food then this is one ingredient that should be high on the list! It adds a subtle flavour to food, and you need only a little at a time so a bottle will last you quite a while.

SERVES 4

1½lb/700g raw beetroot, peeled and grated	1 tablespoon olive oil plus 1 tablespoon very finely chopped walnuts
2 eating apples, sliced (Cox's orange pippins would be good)	2 tablespoons olive oil
	1 tablespoon lemon juice
2oz/50g sultanas, soaked in hot water for 30 minutes	1 teaspoon clear honey
1 tablespoon walnut oil *or*	2 tablespoons yoghurt or mayonnaise

1   Mix together in a large bowl the beetroot, apple and drained sultanas.

2   Combine the walnut oil (or olive oil and chopped walnuts), the olive oil, lemon juice and honey. Pour over the beetroot mixture and mix well. Swirl in the yoghurt or mayonnaise and serve.

Bulgarian Radish and Cheese Salad

This unusual combination can be served as a salad or as a crunchy filling for wholemeal or granary rolls. Radishes are one of the easiest vegetables to grow at home in the smallest of spaces.

SERVES 4

| 8oz/225g radishes (the long variety is milder and easier to grate than the small, round variety) | 2oz/50g Cheddar cheese |
| | 2 tablespoons olive oil |

Grate the radishes and cheese and mix together. Stir in the olive oil and serve.

Pasta Salad

If you eat pasta regularly there will be times when you cook more than you need. This substantial salad is a delicious way of using up the leftovers.

SERVES 4

10oz/275g pasta, cooked
(spirals are best)
2 tablespoons olive oil
1 tablespoon lemon juice
1 tablespoon fresh oregano *or*
1 teaspoon dried oregano
1 tablespoon mayonnaise or
yoghurt
4 small tomatoes, chopped

2 sticks celery, chopped
1 small red pepper, finely
sliced
1 eating apple, diced
1 medium carrot, coarsely
grated
salt and freshly ground black
pepper

1   Put the cooked pasta in a bowl and pour over the olive oil, lemon juice and oregano. (If you have cooked the pasta specially for the salad, do this while it is still warm, and leave to cool.)

2   Add the mayonnaise or yoghurt to the cooled pasta, and then the remaining ingredients. Mix well, season with salt and pepper and serve.

Aubergine Salad

Although this traditional Greek dish is usually cooked on a charcoal fire it is easy to cook at home in a standard oven. The aubergines become delectably sweet with a slightly smoky flavour, and can be eaten simply, with pitta bread, as part of a meal with other dishes, or with cooked rice or pasta.

SERVES 4

2 large aubergines
juice of 1 large lemon
1 red onion, finely chopped
salt

olive oil
2 tablespoons chopped fresh
 parsley

1 Prick the skins of the aubergines and then bake in the oven at 350°C/180°C/gas mark 4, until the aubergines are cooked all the way through and the skins are black. The time this takes will depend on the thickness and size of the aubergines, but allow at least 30 minutes.

2 Slit the cooked aubergines lengthwise and then scoop out all the cooked flesh into a bowl, discarding the skins.

3 Mash the aubergine well with the lemon juice, and then add the chopped onion and a little salt. Mix in the oil drop by drop until a smooth purée is formed, adding as much or as little oil as necessary to get the consistency you would like. Serve sprinkled with chopped parsley.

Winter Leek Salad

Serve this as a salad or as a light meal with toast or plain pasta.

SERVES 4

8 small leeks
2 tablespoons olive oil
1 teaspoon red wine vinegar
1 teaspoon sherry wine vinegar
1 teaspoon concentrated apple
   juice or clear honey

1 teaspoon dried oregano
freshly ground black pepper
2oz/50g almonds, finely
   chopped

1   Clean the leeks by slitting them lengthwise along half their length and running them under cold water to remove the dirt. Cut into 2in/5cm lengths. Simmer the leeks in a little water for 5 minutes, until just cooked. Drain well.

2   Mix together the oil, vinegars, apple juice or honey, oregano and a little black pepper. Pour over the leeks while they are still warm.

3   Sprinkle with the almonds and serve warm or cold.

Crunchy Cauliflower Salad

SERVES 4

1 small cauliflower
2 tablespoons olive oil
1oz/25g hazelnuts, finely
   chopped
1 tablespoon cider vinegar

1 teaspoon clear honey
2 tablespoons chopped fresh
   parsley
freshly ground black pepper

1   Cut the cauliflower into small florets. Either leave the cauliflower raw and crunchy (in which case you might prefer to cut it into very small pieces) or blanch in a little boiling water for 2–3 minutes to soften it slightly, and drain well.

2   Brown the chopped hazelnuts in the oil over a medium heat. Remove from the heat and allow the oil and the nuts to cool.

3   Mix together the cooled nuts and oil, cider vinegar, honey, black pepper and parsley. Pour over the cauliflower, mix carefully and serve.

Late July Salad

This simple salad uses all that is best in the vegetable garden at this time of year. Any salad leaves will do; look out for red oak-leaf lettuce or other unusual salad 'greens'. Serve with Crisp-fried Goats' Cheese, page 122.

SERVES 4

several handfuls of mixed
    lettuce leaves
4–6 young carrots, grated
a handful of lightly steamed
    young French beans
1 large apple, finely sliced
3–4 large sprigs fresh mint

1 large sprig fresh oregano *or* 1
    teaspoon dried oregano
juice of half a lemon
2 tablespoons olive oil
2 teaspoons concentrated
    apple juice or clear honey
freshly ground black pepper

1   Mix together the lettuce, grated carrots, French beans, apple and herbs.

2   Combine the lemon juice, olive oil, apple juice or honey, and black pepper to taste. Sprinkle over the salad ingredients, mix well and serve immediately.

Carrot and Red Onion Salad

Red onions are ideal for eating raw in salads, being much milder and sweeter than the brown-skinned variety. Spring onions make a good substitute.

SERVES 4

4 large carrots, grated
1 red onion, very finely
  chopped
2 eating apples, diced
4 tablespoons yoghurt

1 tablespoon olive oil
2 teaspoons cider vinegar
2 teaspoons concentrated
  apple juice

1   Mix together the carrot, onion and apple.

2   Make a dressing from the yoghurt, olive oil, cider vinegar and apple juice. Mix well with the carrot mixture and serve.

Tabouli

This traditional Lebanese salad uses bulgar wheat (see page 121) and lots of parsley, making it a lovely speckly green colour. It makes a wholesome, fresh lunch and an ideal side salad for a flan or an omelette.

SERVES 4

10oz/275g bulgar wheat
1 teaspoon salt
2 tablespoons olive oil
1 tablespoon lemon juice
2 cloves garlic, crushed
4 large tomatoes, chopped

½ cucumber, diced
3 tablespoons chopped fresh
  mint
4–5 tablespoons chopped
  fresh parsley

1   Put the bulgar wheat and salt into a large bowl, and pour in enough boiling water so that the water is about ½in/1cm above the level of the wheat. Leave to stand for about 10 minutes, stirring from time to time.

2   Drain off any excess liquid – there should be very little, if any. Mix the olive oil, lemon juice and garlic into the warm bulgar wheat and allow to cool.

3   Add the tomatoes, cucumber and herbs and mix well before serving.

Greek Salad

Look for good, flavourful tomatoes and authentic Feta cheese for this recipe (Feta cheese ready-marinated in olive oil and herbs has the best flavour). Not all versions of Greek Salad include lettuce, but you will find that the lettuce helps to soak up all the delicious juices.

SERVES 4

1 small head of crunchy lettuce (for example Cos or Webbs)
6 large tomatoes
1 medium cucumber
2 small green or red peppers
1 small red onion
a handful of black olives
4oz/110g Feta cheese
fresh or dried oregano to taste
3–4fl oz/75–100ml olive oil
a dash of red wine vinegar

1   Finely chop the lettuce, slice the tomatoes, cucumber and peppers. Slice the onion into very fine rings.

2   Line the base of a large bowl with the lettuce. Add the tomatoes, cucumber, peppers and onion and then the olives and the crumbled Feta cheese. Scatter with a handful of chopped fresh oregano or a little dried oregano. Sprinkle over the olive oil and the vinegar, mix very gently and serve.

Spicy Bananas

An unusual salad idea to spice up a meal. Look out for quite ripe bananas, which are often a bargain, but ensure that they are not overripe and becoming too soft.

SERVES 4

4 large ripe bananas
juice of half a lemon
2 tablespoons yoghurt
2 tablespoons olive oil

2 teaspoons clear honey
1–2 tablespoons mild curry
  powder

1   Peel and slice the bananas thickly and sprinkle with the lemon juice.

2   Mix together the yoghurt, olive oil, honey and curry powder (add more curry powder if you like a hotter, spicier flavour). Carefully coat the bananas with the yoghurt dressing and serve.

Small Vegetable Dishes

Serve two or three of these vegetable dishes in combination to make a main meal, or serve as a side dish with one of the recipes in the Main Dishes section. Some will also make a good light lunch or supper served with a simple salad or some crusty bread.

Carrots and Chilli

Apple juice is very useful for cooking carrots as it enhances their natural sweetness.

SERVES 4

2 tablespoons olive oil
1 onion, finely sliced into rings
1 clove garlic, crushed
1 small red chilli, deseeded and chopped very finely

1lb/450g carrots, cut into fine sticks
5fl oz/150ml apple juice

1   Heat the oil in a pan over a medium heat. Add the onion, garlic and chilli and cook gently for 5–10 minutes, until the onion is well softened.

2   Add the carrots and apple juice, bring to the boil, cover and simmer gently for about 5–10 minutes, until the carrots are just cooked. Add a little extra water if it is needed to stop the carrots becoming too dry.

Aubergine Fritters

This is a wonderful way to cook aubergines: long thin slices are fried quickly until crisp, leaving the insides soft and juicy. Serve this as a simple accompaniment to a main dish or as an easy starter with a little tzatziki (page 133). Be generous with the lemon as its sharpness really enhances the flavours.

SERVES 4

2 large aubergines
2 eggs
wholemeal flour for coating
freshly ground black pepper

light oil for frying (sunflower is good)
2 lemons

1   Slice the aubergines from top to bottom in thin slices no more than ¼in/5mm thick. If you wish, you can salt the slices and leave them to 'de-gorge' for 20–30 minutes to remove some of the bitter juices. Then rinse the slices and dry with a tea towel. Although this process is often recommended with aubergines, I don't think it makes much difference to the end result, so don't bother with it if you don't want to.

2   Beat the eggs. Dip the aubergine slices into the egg and then coat with the flour seasoned with black pepper.

3   Heat the oil in a large frying pan and then fry the aubergine slices, several at a time, on both sides until crisp and brown. Keep warm until all are cooked then serve with 2 quarters of lemon per person.

Spiced Parsnips

For greater energy efficiency, if you are not using the oven to cook any other dishes, finish cooking the parsnips at stage 2 on top of the cooker.

SERVES 4

2 tablespoons olive oil
1 teaspoon coriander seeds
1 teaspoon ground ginger
1 medium onion, sliced
1 medium carrot, finely sliced
1lb/450g parsnips, finely sliced

5fl oz/150ml apple juice or
  water
2 bay leaves
salt and freshly ground black
  pepper

1   Heat the oil in a flameproof casserole, add the coriander seed and the ginger and cook over a medium heat for 5 minutes. Add the onion, carrot and parsnips and cook for a further 5 minutes.

2   Pour over the apple juice or water, add the bay leaves and bring to the boil. Cover the casserole and bake in a moderate oven, 375°F/190°C/gas mark 5, for about 30 minutes. Season with salt and pepper before serving.

Stir-fried Sprouts

Brussels sprouts are a much-maligned vegetable so often spoilt by over-cooking. Stir-frying is one way to ensure that you do not over-cook and ruin your sprouts.

SERVES 4

2 tablespoons sunflower oil	3–4 tomatoes, sliced
1 onion, finely chopped	1 teaspoon wholegrain
1lb/450g small Brussels	mustard or Dijon mustard *or*
sprouts	1 tablespoon walnut oil

1   In a large, heavy pan or a wok heat the oil over a medium heat. Add the onion and cook for 4–5 minutes.

2   Add the sprouts and the tomatoes and cook for a further 8–10 minutes, stirring frequently. Add a little water if the mixture seems dry. You can speed up the cooking by covering the pan and trapping in the steam.

3   When the sprouts are just cooked, remove from the heat and add the mustard or walnut oil, stirring to mix in well.

Spanish Courgettes

Courgettes abound in greengrocers and markets in mid to late summer. Equally, if you grow courgettes with any degree of success then you are likely to have a large crop and will welcome new ideas for cooking them. This one would go well with an egg or cheese dish or would make a light lunch dish with some plain buttery noodles.

SERVES 4

2 tablespoons olive oil
8 courgettes, thickly sliced
8 tomatoes, thickly sliced
4 cloves garlic, chopped
8 black olives, stoned and
   halved

1 tablespoon chopped fresh
   basil *or* 1 teaspoon dried
   basil
freshly ground black pepper

Heat the olive oil in a pan. Add all remaining ingredients, cover the pan and cook over a moderate heat for 15–20 minutes, stirring from time to time. Add a little water during cooking if the mixture seems dry. If you are using the oven to cook other dishes at the same time then you can also cook this in the oven, in a covered casserole.

Fast Courgettes

Another recipe for the summer glut of courgettes – a crisp yet moist accompaniment that goes well with pasta or egg dishes.

SERVES 4

2 tablespoons olive oil
2oz/50g flaked almonds
1lb/450g courgettes, finely
   sliced
juice of half a lemon

1   Heat the oil in a large pan. Add the almonds and the courgettes and cook over a moderate heat for 5–10 minutes, until the almonds and courgettes are browned. Turn the heat up high for the last minute to crisp the courgettes.

2   Remove from the heat, stir in the lemon juice and serve.

Sweet and Sour Leeks

Leeks are good to grow at home, as they take up so little space in your garden. They will see you through the winter and can be used in many ways – even as a good alternative to the ubiquitous onion. Here they are enjoyed in their own right in another quick-cooking dish. Serve with rice or mashed potato for a light meal, or as a side dish in a larger meal.

SERVES 4

8 medium leeks (avoid the
    large, rather watery ones)
2 tablespoons olive oil
1 red pepper, cut into thin
    strips
1 tablespoon cornflour

½ pint/275ml water
1 tablespoon clear honey
1 tablespoon shoyu
1 tablespoon tomato purée
1 tablespoon red wine vinegar

1   Slit the leeks lengthwise along two-thirds of their length and run under cold water to clean out the dirt. Cut into 2in/5cm chunks.

2   Heat the oil in a pan, add the leeks and the pepper, and cook for 8–10 minutes over a medium heat, until the leeks begin to soften.

3   Mix the cornflour with 2–3 tablespoons of the water and then stir in the rest of the water. Add the honey, shoyu, tomato purée and vinegar. Pour over the leeks and cook for a further 3–5 minutes, until the sauce thickens and the leeks are coated in the sauce.

Mushrooms with Cumin and Lemon

Choose organic brown cap mushrooms for the best flavour and texture, and look for unwaxed lemons when using lemon rind in cooking.

SMALL VEGETABLE DISHES   85

SERVES 4

12oz/350g mushrooms	1 teaspoon cumin seeds
2–3 tablespoons olive oil	grated rind and juice of 1
2 cloves garlic, crushed	lemon

1   Cut the mushrooms into quarters if they are large; if they are small leave them whole.

2   Heat the olive oil in a large pan, add the garlic and cumin seed and cook over a low heat for 2–3 minutes. Turn up the heat to medium and add the mushrooms. Cook for a further 5–10 minutes, stirring well. Add the lemon rind and juice and serve.

Roast Jerusalem Artichokes

Roast these artichokes in the oven alongside a main dish, such as Tortilla Pie (page 101) or Mackerel with Shallots and Tomatoes (page 136). Or serve them in place of roast potatoes – their interesting, smoky flavour complements traditional dishes well.

SERVES 4

1lb/450g Jerusalem artichokes
1–2 tablespoons olive oil
juice of half a lemon

1   Scrub the artichokes well and cut any large ones into smaller pieces. Arrange on an oiled baking tray and brush the tops of the artichokes with the remaining oil.

2   Bake in a hot oven, 400°F/200°C/gas mark 6, for about 30 minutes, until soft inside. Remove from the oven and sprinkle with the lemon juice before serving.

French Peas

Choose fresh peas if you can and for the best flavour cook as soon as possible after buying them. Better still, grow your own.

SERVES 4

1 tablespoon olive oil	1 tablespoon chopped fresh
2 medium onions, sliced into	thyme *or* 1 teaspoon dried
fine rings	thyme
1 clove garlic, crushed	1 tablespoon chopped fresh
10oz/275g peas, fresh or frozen	mint *or* 1 teaspoon dried
1 small lettuce *or* a few leaves	mint
from a garden lettuce,	salt and freshly ground black
chopped	pepper

1   Heat the olive oil in a pan, add the onions and garlic and cook over a moderate heat for 5–10 minutes, until very soft.

2   Add the peas and the lettuce with the thyme and mint. Cover the pan and continue to cook gently for a further 5–10 minutes, until the peas are cooked. Fresh peas will take longer than frozen. If you wish, season with salt and black pepper to taste before serving.

Warm Celery with Cream Cheese

This could be served as a first course, a light main course or as a special side dish. Organic soft cheese is quite widely available and worth seeking out.

SERVES 4

3–4 sticks celery	1 clove garlic, crushed
4oz/110g cream, curd or soft	freshly ground black pepper
cheese	2 tablespoons chopped chives

1   Cut the sticks of celery into eight 3in/7.5cm lengths. Blanch in a little boiling water for 4–5 minutes, until the celery is just beginning to soften. Drain and cool slightly.

2   Cream the cheese with the garlic and a little pepper.

3   Arrange the celery pieces in an ovenproof serving dish and fill with the cream cheese. Place under a medium grill for 3–5 minutes, until the cheese begins to melt. Sprinkle with the chopped chives and serve.

Balkan Red Cabbage

Although this lovely red vegetable dish is best baked in the oven, if you are not using the oven for any other dish then it may be more energy efficient to cook it on top of the cooker, in a pan with a tightly fitting lid.

SERVES 4

1½lb/700g red cabbage, shredded	1 large apple, finely sliced
1 large onion, finely sliced	½ pint/275ml apple juice
	3 tablespoons red wine vinegar

Layer the red cabbage, onion and apple in a casserole. Pour over the apple juice and red wine vinegar. Cover the casserole and bake in a medium oven, 350°F/180°C/gas mark 4, for about 1 hour.

Alternatively, put the cabbage, onion and apple into a large pan and add the apple juice and vinegar. Bring to the boil, cover tightly and then simmer very gently for 15–20 minutes. Remove the lid and if necessary reduce the liquid by turning the heat up for 1–2 minutes before serving.

Chinese Egg Rice

This fried rice intertwined with crisp omelette strips makes a substantial accompaniment to a vegetable stir-fry (page 114). It uses plain cooked rice, so is a good opportunity for cooking more rice than you need and refrigerating some of it for another dish, or for using leftover rice from the previous meal. Use long-grain brown rice rather than white rice – the flavour is superior, it is much easier to cook and of course is the 'green' choice, having gone through less processing. It also contains more vitamins and minerals, especially B vitamins. In addition, organic brown rice is now widely available, whereas organic white rice is more difficult to find.

SERVES 4

2 pints/1.1 litre water
1lb/450g long-grain brown rice
2½ tablespoons sunflower oil
1 egg beaten with 1 tablespoon water

1 small mild onion or 2 spring onions, finely chopped
salt or shoyu and freshly ground black pepper

1   Bring the water to boil in a large pan. Add the rice, bring to the boil, cover and simmer very gently for 25 minutes until the rice is cooked and the liquid has been absorbed. If not quite all the liquid has been absorbed then drain it off.

2   Heat ½ tablespoon of the oil in a large frying-pan over a high heat. Add the beaten egg, tip the pan to allow the egg to cover the base and cook the omelette until set. Remove from the pan and cut into thin strips.

3   Put the remaining oil into the pan over a medium heat and add the onion. Cook for 3–5 minutes and then add the rice. Cook for 8–10 minutes, stirring well, until the rice begins to brown. If necessary, turn up the heat slightly. As the rice begins to brown add the omelette strips, season with salt or shoyu and black pepper and serve immediately.

Potatoes from Crete

Potatoes cooked with local herbs and tomatoes are a popular dish on the menus of tavernas in Crete – the potatoes are a perfect vehicle for all the pungent flavours. Use mild, sweet flavoured red onions if you can for this dish; otherwise use ordinary onions, making sure they are well cooked in the first stage of the recipe. If you are using the oven for other dishes cook this alongside them; if not, it will do equally well, and economically, on top of the cooker.

SERVES 4

2 tablespoons olive oil
2 red onions, sliced into fine
   rings
5 cloves garlic, chopped
1 red pepper, chopped
8oz/225g tomatoes, chopped
8 medium potatoes, cut into
   small chunks

1 teaspoon dried marjoram
1 teaspoon dried mint
salt and freshly ground black
   pepper
5fl oz/150ml water

1   Heat the oil in a large flameproof casserole, add the onion, garlic, pepper and tomatoes, cover and cook gently over a medium heat for 7–8 minutes.

2   Add the potatoes, marjoram, mint, salt and pepper, and the water. Cover and place in the centre of a moderate oven, 350°F/180°C/gas mark 4, for 40–50 minutes, until the potatoes are cooked. Alternatively, leave to cook gently on top of the cooker for about 25–30 minutes, stirring from time to time to prevent sticking.

Bubble and Squeak

Good for using leftover mashed potato and cooked greens, Bubble
and Squeak is both traditional and a superb dish in its own right.
Any type of greens works in this recipe, apart from curly kale which
you may find overpowering. Try Brussels sprout tops, available in
supermarkets and excellent value, the sprouts themselves, Savoy
cabbage or spring greens. Serve with Barbecue Burgers (page 130)
and a good wholegrain mustard.

SERVES 4

2 tablespoons olive oil
1 small onion, finely chopped
8oz/225g cabbage-type greens,
   cooked and chopped

1½lb/700g potatoes, cooked
   and mashed
salt and freshly ground black
   pepper

1   Heat the oil in a large, heavy frying-pan, add the onion and cook
over a medium heat for 2–3 minutes.

2   Add the greens, cook for 2–3 minutes, and then add the mashed
potato. Season with salt and pepper to taste, press down well and
cook for 5 minutes until the underneath starts to brown. Roughly
turn the potato mixture over in the pan and continue to cook for
another 10 minutes, turning occasionally to brown as much of the
potato as possible. Add a little extra oil during cooking if necessary.
You may need to raise the heat to high towards the end of cooking
to get the potato really brown.

Latkes

These potato cakes made with grated raw potato look attractive, and are soft on the inside and lovely and crisp on the outside. Serve with a moist vegetable dish, such as Summer Stew (page 104), or with Braised Rabbit (page 143).

SERVES 4

8 large potatoes
2 onions
2 eggs, beaten
2oz/50g fine wholemeal flour

salt and freshly ground black
  pepper
2–3 tablespoons olive oil

1   Peel and grate the potatoes (leave the skin on if they are organic) and dry the grated potato with a tea towel. Grate the onions and mix with the potatoes in a large bowl. Mix in the eggs and the flour and season well.

2   Heat the oil in a large pan over a medium heat. Drop spoonfuls of the mixture into the oil and cook for about 5 minutes, until golden on one side; then turn and brown the other side. The potato should be soft all the way through.

Variation To make these little potato cakes more of a meal in themselves add 3oz/75g grated Cheddar cheese to the mixture before frying.

Lemon Rice

This simple, spicy lemon rice is a much more interesting accompaniment than boiled rice for curries, casseroles, egg or cheese dishes. Make double the quantity and reheat it or eat it cold for lunch with a salad (it will keep for about 24 hours in the fridge).

SERVES 4

2 tablespoons olive oil
2 onions, cut into small chunks
2 cloves garlic, chopped
1 teaspoon cumin seed
2 teaspoons garam masala
1 teaspoon turmeric
8oz/225g long-grain brown rice
1 pint/570ml boiling water
1 bay leaf
2oz/50g peas (optional)
grated rind and juice of 1 lemon
salt and freshly ground black pepper

1   Heat the oil in a large pan over a moderate heat, and add the onions, garlic, cumin seed, garam masala and turmeric. Cook for 5 minutes, stirring constantly.

2   Stir in the washed rice and fry for a minute with the onions and spices. Add the boiling water and the bay leaf. Bring to the boil, stir once and then cover the pan and simmer gently for 20–30 minutes until the rice is cooked and the water has been absorbed. Add the peas, if using, during the last 5 minutes of cooking.

3   When the rice is cooked, add the lemon rind and juice, season with salt and black pepper and serve.

Gratin of French Beans

French beans bring to mind summer, with their lovely green colour and sweet flavour. Grow your own or buy them from a pick-your-own farm for perfect freshness – choose the small beans as these are the most tender. Serve this gratin as a side dish or as a light meal with a salad.

SERVES 4

1lb/450g French beans	2oz/50g breadcrumbs
1oz/25g butter or margarine	1 tablespoon olive oil
2 large tomatoes, chopped	2oz/50g Cheddar cheese,
2 cloves garlic, crushed	grated

1   Cook the beans in a little boiling water until *al dente*. Drain and keep warm in a shallow ovenproof dish.

2   Melt the butter in a small pan, add the tomatoes and garlic and cook for 3–4 minutes. Pour over the beans.

3   Mix together the breadcrumbs, olive oil and Cheddar cheese. Sprinkle over the French beans and put under the grill for a few minutes to brown the breadcrumbs and melt the cheese.

Crispy Swede Bake

This bake can be served with one or two other simple vegetable dishes from this section to make up a meal, or as an accompaniment to a main course dish.

SERVES 4

1 large swede, weighing about
   2lb/1 kilo

salt and freshly ground black
   pepper

Topping

1 small onion, finely chopped
2 cloves garlic, crushed
2oz/50g Cheddar cheese,
   grated

1 large tomato, chopped
1 teaspoon dried marjoram
3oz/75g porridge oats
2 tablespoons sunflower oil

1   Peel the swede, cut into small chunks and boil in plenty of water in a covered pan until tender – this can take up to 30 minutes. Drain and mash with a little salt and pepper. Put into an ovenproof dish.

2   Mix together the topping ingredients and spoon over the mashed swede. Bake in a moderate oven, 375°F/190°C/gas mark 5, for 25 minutes. If you do not wish to use the oven, put the dish under a medium grill for 10 minutes, stirring the topping round once or twice during this time to prevent it burning.

Main Dishes

The recipes here are for vegetarian main course dishes. They are all easy to prepare and use ingredients that should be readily available even if only seasonally. Many of these dishes are quite quick to cook, others can cook slowly in the oven together with an accompaniment, perhaps simply jacket potatoes.

Hunter's Casserole

Red split lentils cook quickly and give substance and protein to this tasty casserole.

SERVES 4

2 tablespoons olive oil
1 medium onion, roughly
    chopped
6oz/175g button mushrooms,
    cut into quarters
2 sticks celery, chopped
6 cloves garlic, chopped
5fl oz/150ml creamed
    tomatoes or *passata*

1 teaspoon dried marjoram
1 tablespoon shoyu
4oz/110g red split lentils
2oz/50g hazelnuts
8fl oz/200ml water
3 tablespoons grated Parmesan
    cheese

1   Put the oil into a flameproof casserole over a medium heat and add the onion, mushrooms, celery and garlic. Cover and cook for 5 minutes.

2   Add the creamed tomatoes, marjoram, shoyu, lentils, hazelnuts and water. Bring to the boil, cover and simmer for about 30 minutes, adding a little extra water if necessary to prevent the casserole from becoming too dry. Stir in the Parmesan and simmer for a further 10 minutes or so.

Suffolk Hot-Pot

Use whatever vegetables you have for this warming winter dish.

SERVES 4

2–3 tablespoons olive oil
2 medium onions, chopped
4 cloves garlic, chopped
2 large carrots, chopped
2 parsnips, chopped
1 stick celery, chopped
3 small leeks, chopped
3 large potatoes, sliced into thin rings
4 large tomatoes, chopped
3oz/75g Cheddar cheese, grated or Feta or goats' cheese, crumbled

6 large mushrooms, cut in half
1 teaspoon dried thyme
1 teaspoon dried marjoram
freshly ground black pepper
2 tablespoons tomato purée, dissolved in ½ pint/275ml water
2 tablespoons olive paste (see page 165) or 10 black olives, stoned and very finely chopped

1   Heat the oil in a large flameproof casserole over a medium heat. Add the onions, garlic, carrots, parsnips, celery and leeks and cook gently for 10 minutes. Take off the heat and remove the vegetables from the casserole.

2   Arrange a layer of potato slices in the bottom of the casserole. Sprinkling the herbs and black pepper over the layers as they are added, cover the potato slices with half of the vegetable mixture, then another layer of potatoes, and then the tomatoes, cheese and mushrooms. Cover with the rest of the vegetable mixture and finish with a layer of potatoes.

3   Mix the tomato purée and water with the olive paste or chopped olives. Pour over the vegetables. Brush the top layer of potatoes with a little extra olive oil. Cover and cook in a moderate oven, 375°F/190°C/gas mark 5, for about 1 hour, removing the lid for the last 20 minutes to brown the potatoes.

Warming Chestnut Casserole

Chesnuts, available in dried form from wholefood shops, make substantial, warming meals, and their excellent flavour and firm texture are particularly successful with hardened meat-eaters! This casserole, like most of the stews and casseroles in this book, can be cooked on top of the cooker or in the oven, if you are already using the oven for other dishes.

SERVES 4

8oz/225g dried chestnuts	3 medium potatoes, sliced into chunks
2 pints/1.1 litre water	1½ teaspoons dried sage
2 tablespoons olive oil	1½ teaspoons dried thyme
4 small carrots, sliced	1½ tablespoons wholemeal flour
2 small leeks, sliced	2 tablespoons shoyu
8oz/225g celeriac, diced or 4 sticks celery, chopped	1½ tablespoons cider vinegar
8oz/225g mushrooms, quartered if large	

1   Put the chestnuts into a large pan with the water. Bring to the boil, cover the pan and simmer gently for 30 minutes, until the chestnuts are just soft. Remove from the heat.

2   Heat the olive oil in a large, flameproof casserole, and add the carrots, leeks, celeriac or celery, mushrooms, potatoes, sage and thyme. Cover the casserole and cook the vegetables over a medium heat for 5–10 minutes.

3   Sprinkle in the flour, stirring well, and add the chestnuts and their cooking liquid. Bring to the boil, stirring constantly. Add the shoyu and the cider vinegar, cover the casserole and cook in a 375°F/190°C/gas mark 5 oven for 30–45 minutes, until the vegetables are tender.

Alternatively, continue to simmer the casserole gently on top of the cooker. Check the casserole from time to time and add a little extra water if necessary.

A Choice of Pies

The beauty of this recipe is that you can use whatever combination of vegetables you have and, of course, you can include vegetables left over from an earlier meal. When choosing the vegetables remember to think about the colour and texture as well as flavour. For example, make sure that you brighten up a selection of root vegetables by including a bright red pepper or some peas or French beans. There are four ideas for 'lids' on pages 99–101: a wholemeal pastry, a cheese cobbler, a nutty crumble or a crispy potato topping.

SERVES 4

Filling

2lb/900g mixed vegetables –
carrots, leeks, cauliflower,
sweetcorn, aubergines,
courgettes, peppers, celery,
peas, broccoli, swede,
parsnips, cabbage,
mushrooms, shallots, onions,
etc.
2oz/50g margarine
1½oz/40g wholemeal flour

15fl oz/400ml milk
1 tablespoon chopped fresh
thyme *or* 1 teaspoon dried
thyme
4 tablespoons chopped fresh
parsley
2 bay leaves
shoyu or salt and freshly
ground black pepper

1   Prepare and dice the vegetables.

2   Put a little water into a large pan (enough to make a depth of 1in/2.5cm in the pan), bring to the boil and add the vegetables, starting with the ones which need longer to cook. Cover and steam the vegetables until just cooked. Make sure that the pan does not boil dry and also take care not to overcook the vegetables – they should still be a little crunchy. Drain if necessary and put into a deep-sided pie dish.

3   Melt the margarine in a small pan over a medium heat and add the flour. Cook gently for 2–3 minutes and remove from the heat.

Gradually incorporate the milk, stirring briskly. Return to the heat and bring to the boil, stirring until the sauce boils and thickens. Add the thyme, parsley and bay leaves, season with a little shoyu or salt and pepper. Pour over the vegetables in the pie dish and mix together carefully.

4   Cover with one of the toppings on pages 99–101 and follow the instructions for baking.

Casserole and Pie Toppings

Use any one of these toppings for the pie recipe on page 98, or to transform one of the vegetable or bean dishes into a more elaborate supper dish.

Wholemeal Pastry Lid

8oz/225g fine wholemeal flour
a pinch of salt
a pinch of baking powder
2oz/50g margarine, chilled, or

white vegetable fat, or a
combination of both
a little cold water

1   Sieve the flour, salt and baking powder into a large bowl. Add the margarine or fat and rub in lightly until the mixture resembles breadcrumbs.

2   Add 3–4 tablespoons of cold water and, using a knife, mix into the crumbs. Draw together the dough with your fingertips – it should be moist enough to come together easily. Knead lightly and form into a ball, cover and leave to rest in the fridge for 10 minutes.

3   Roll out thinly on a lightly floured board. Brush the edges of the pie dish with a little milk and cover with the pastry, pressing down the edges well. Trim off the extra pastry, and use to make simple decorations for the top. Using a sharp knife, cut an air hole in the centre, brush with milk and bake in a hot oven, 400°F/200°C/gas mark 6, for about 25 minutes, until golden brown.

Cheese Cobbler Topping

6oz/175g fine wholemeal flour
1 teaspoon baking powder
a pinch of salt
½ teaspoon mustard powder
2oz/50g margarine

3oz/75g Cheddar cheese,
   grated
1 egg
a little milk

1   Sift the flour, baking powder, salt and mustard powder into a large bowl. Rub in the margarine and add the cheese, mixing well.

2   Beat the egg and add to the flour with sufficient milk to make a moist dough. Roll out on a lightly floured board. Cover the pie dish with the dough, pressing down the edges well. Alternatively, cut out circles of dough with a large pastry cutter and lay the circles edge to edge on top of the vegetable or bean mixture. Bake at 400°F/200°C/gas mark 6 for about 20 minutes, until browned.

Nutty Crumble

4oz/110g wholemeal
   breadcrumbs
2oz/50g hazelnuts, finely
   chopped

1 teaspoon dried marjoram or
   oregano
3 tablespoons olive oil

1   Mix together all the ingredients and sprinkle on top of the vegetables.

2   Bake in a moderate oven, 375°F/190°C/gas mark 5, for 15–20 minutes. Alternatively, if the vegetables are still hot, put under a low-to-medium grill for 10 minutes until crisp and brown, taking care not to burn the top.

Potato Topping

1½lb/700g potatoes
2oz/50g margarine
2–3 tablespoons milk

salt and freshly ground black
   pepper

1   Cook the unpeeled potatoes in boiling water until just soft. Drain. Mash or purée the potatoes with the margarine and the milk, and season with salt and pepper.

2   Cover the vegetable or bean mixture with the potato. Dot a little extra margarine on top and bake in the oven at 375°F/190°C/gas mark 5 for 20 minutes. Alternatively, if the vegetables are still hot, finish cooking the pie by putting it under a medium grill for 5–10 minutes, taking care that it does not burn.

Tortilla Pie

A giant omelette that is baked in the oven – much easier than making individual omelettes on the hob if you are cooking for several people.

SERVES 4

2 tablespoons olive oil
1 large onion, sliced into fine rings
1 small red pepper, sliced into fine rings
1 small green pepper, sliced into fine rings
2 cloves garlic, chopped
1 teaspoon dried oregano
6–8 black olives, stoned and roughly chopped
6 eggs
4 tablespoons water
4oz/110g Cheddar cheese, grated
freshly ground black pepper

1   Put the olive oil in a pan over a medium heat, add the onion, peppers and garlic, cover and fry gently for 10 minutes. Stir in the oregano and olives and spoon into a large, shallow ovenproof dish.

2   Beat the eggs with the water, most of the cheese and black pepper to taste. Pour over the vegetables in the dish and sprinkle the remaining cheese over the top.

3   Bake in the oven at 400°F/200°C/gas mark 6 for 20–30 minutes, until the eggs are set and the top is brown and bubbling. Serve hot, straight from the oven.

Country Bean Stew

Bean stews can be wonderfully rich and satisfying. They do take some time to prepare, though, so make plenty to serve in different ways for several meals – with jacket potatoes cooked in the oven at the same time, or with a pastry, cobbler or potato topping (pages 99–101). They also freeze successfully. If you prefer, use ready-cooked tinned beans. Haricot or butter beans can also be substituted for cannellini beans, depending on what is most easily available. Don't worry about the 15 cloves of garlic – since they are left whole they simply give the beans a subtle aromatic flavour rather than an obvious garlic taste.

SERVES 4

8oz/225g dried cannellini beans *or* 1 14oz/400g tin cooked cannellini beans
2 tablespoons olive oil
2 large onions, sliced into fine rings
15 small cloves garlic, left whole
2 green peppers, roughly chopped
4oz/110g mushrooms, cut into quarters

1 eating apple, sliced
6 tomatoes, chopped
½ pint/275ml creamed tomatoes or *passata*
1 tablespoon shoyu
1 tablespoon concentrated apple juice
1 teaspoon dried thyme
2 bay leaves
freshly ground black pepper

1   If you are using dried beans put them in a bowl, cover with boiling water and leave to soak for 1 hour. Drain, put in a pan, cover with fresh water and bring to the boil. Boil rapidly for 10 minutes, then cover the pan and simmer gently for 20–30 minutes until the beans are just beginning to soften. Drain and set aside.

2   Heat the oil in a large flameproof casserole. Add the onions, garlic cloves, peppers and mushrooms and cook over a medium heat for 10 minutes. Add the apple and tomatoes, and the beans (drain and rinse tinned beans first if using these). Mix in the

creamed tomatoes, shoyu, apple juice, thyme, bay leaves, and black pepper to taste. Cover, bring to the boil and then transfer to the oven, 350°F/180°C/gas mark 4, for 1–1½ hours, until the beans are well cooked or for 40 minutes if you are using tinned beans. Add a little extra water during cooking if necessary.

Note   If you are not using the oven for another dish, you can continue cooking the casserole on top of the cooker, in which case you will need to cook it for only 45 minutes or so. A pressure cooker would reduce both the time for the initial cooking of the beans and for cooking the stew, but it is easy to overcook the dish in a pressure cooker, making the beans break up and turn mushy.

Scrambled Vegetables

This is a version of the French dish *Pipérade*, and is best made with good quality free-range eggs. Serve with jacket potatoes, or more simply with hot buttered toast.

SERVES 4

2oz/50g butter or vegetable
  margarine
2 carrots, grated
3 leeks, finely shredded
4 cloves garlic, chopped
4 tomatoes, skinned and
  roughly chopped

2oz/50g pecan nuts, chopped
6 eggs, beaten
salt and freshly ground black
  pepper

1   Melt the butter in a large heavy pan over a medium heat. Add the carrots, leeks and garlic, cover and cook gently for 5–10 minutes.

2   Add the tomatoes and the nuts. Stir in the eggs, season with salt and pepper, and cook, stirring continuously, until the eggs are cooked but still soft. Serve immediately.

Summer Stew

This quickly cooked dish makes a tasty main meal served with lots of tagliatelle. It is also good served on crisply toasted bread as a lunch or supper dish. The pungent flavour of the sherry wine vinegar adds a touch of luxury. If you do not have this, use a medium dry sherry instead.

SERVES 4

2 tablespoons olive oil
1 large aubergine, diced
2 large courgettes, diced
3 cloves garlic, chopped
2 teaspoons sherry wine
    vinegar
8oz/225g mushrooms, roughly
    chopped if large

12oz/350g fresh, ripe tomatoes
    or *passata* (bottled,
    ready-sieved tomatoes)
3 tablespoons natural yoghurt
salt and freshly ground black
    pepper

1   Heat the oil in a large pan, add the aubergine, courgettes, garlic and sherry wine vinegar and cook over a moderate heat for 5 minutes. Add the mushrooms and cook for a further 5 minutes, stirring occasionally.

2   If using fresh tomatoes, skin and chop finely. Add the tomatoes or the *passata* to the vegetables, with a little water if the mixture seems dry. Cover the pan and continue cooking for a further 10 minutes. Remove from the heat and season to taste with salt and pepper.

3   Spoon the yoghurt over the top, replace the lid and leave to warm through off the heat for 1–2 minutes (this prevents the yoghurt from curdling). Give the mixture a stir and then serve.

The Ultimate Aubergine

This recipe is a combination of several wonderful aubergine dishes – from Imam Bayeldi, a stuffed aubergine recipe from Turkey, to moussaka and caponata. The aubergine is a very versatile vegetable and can now be grown successfully at home in a greenhouse.

SERVES 4

4 medium potatoes, thickly
   sliced
2 tablespoons olive oil
2 onions, chopped
2 cloves garlic, crushed
1 large aubergine, diced
4oz/110g mushrooms, sliced
1 teaspoon curry powder
2 tablespoons tomato purée

1oz/25g breadcrumbs
1oz/25g almonds, roughly
   chopped
1 teaspoon dried mint
12–15fl oz/325–400ml water
a little extra oil
salt and freshly ground black
   pepper

1   Cook the potatoes in boiling water until just soft, drain and keep warm.

2   Meanwhile, heat the oil in a pan, and add the onions, garlic, aubergine, mushrooms and curry powder. Cover and cook gently over a medium heat for 10 minutes. Add the tomato purée, breadcrumbs, almonds, mint and water, stirring to make a smooth mixture. Cook gently for a further 10 minutes and then season with a little salt and pepper

3   Spoon half the aubergine mixture into an ovenproof casserole, add a layer of potato slices, cover with the rest of the aubergine mixture and then finish with the remaining potatoes. Brush the surface of the potatoes with the extra oil and grill under a medium heat for about 5 minutes to brown. Serve.

Mainline Pasta

Pasta has seemingly endless possibilities as a vehicle for all sorts of interesting sauces and fillings. It is also easy, quick-cooking and substantial. Here are just four, very different sauces for your pasta.

You will need about 12oz/350g pasta to serve 4 people, or 3oz/75g per person. Boil for 7–10 minutes in boiling water, then drain well and top with or mix in one of the sauces below.

Ten-Minute Mushroom Sauce

Sherry wine vinegar, a good item for your store cupboard, is what makes this sauce so special. It may seem expensive but you use very little at a time, and its flavour is superb.

SERVES 4

3 tablespoons olive oil
4 cloves garlic, chopped
12oz/350g fresh tomatoes, quartered
1lb/450g mushrooms, quartered

2 tablespoons sherry wine vinegar or medium dry sherry
2 tablespoons shoyu
2 teaspoons dried oregano
freshly ground black pepper

1   Heat the oil in a pan over a medium heat and add the garlic. Cook for 3 minutes. Add the tomatoes and cook for a further 3 minutes.

2   Add the mushrooms and the rest of the ingredients, cover the pan and continue cooking for 5 minutes. Remove the lid and reduce the liquid for 4–5 minutes. Serve on a bed of hot pasta.

Good Tomato Sauce

Tomato sauce is the traditional, ever-popular accompaniment to pasta, served with lots of Parmesan sprinkled on top. Here is a good recipe.

SERVES 4

2 tablespoons olive oil
1 onion, finely chopped
2–3 cloves garlic, crushed
1lb/450g fresh tomatoes, peeled and chopped *or* 1 14oz/400g can of tomatoes, drained and chopped
2 tablespoons tomato purée
1 tablespoon chopped fresh basil
1 tablespoon chopped fresh oregano
1 tablespoon chopped fresh marjoram
} *or* 1 teaspoon each of the dried herb

1 teaspoon brown sugar or concentrated apple juice
salt and freshly ground black pepper
grated Parmesan cheese to serve

1   Heat the oil in a large pan and cook the onion and garlic for 5–10 minutes until soft.

2   Add the tomatoes, tomato purée, herbs and sugar or apple juice, cover the pan and continue to cook for a further 10 minutes, adding a little water (or tomato juice from tinned tomatoes) if the sauce seems dry. Season with salt and pepper. Serve with cooked pasta and sprinkle with plenty of Parmesan.

Black Olive Sauce

SERVES 4

2 tablespoons olive paste,
  home made (see page 163),
  or ready made
1 small onion, finely chopped
2 tablespoons olive oil
8oz/225g tomatoes, peeled and
  chopped *or* 8oz/225g tinned
  tomatoes, drained and
  chopped
5fl oz/150ml single cream or
  smetana
grated Parmesan cheese to
  serve

1   Fry the onion in the oil until soft. Add the tomatoes and cook for a further 5 minutes.

2   Remove from the heat and stir in the olive paste and the cream. Warm through gently, taking care not to boil. Toss the cooked pasta in the sauce and serve with Parmesan sprinkled on top.

Feta Cheese Sauce

This is a dryish sauce and is perfect for coating pasta served as a light first course, or as one of several small dishes to make up a main course.

SERVES 4

2 tablespoons olive oil
1 onion, sliced into rings
1 red pepper, sliced into rings
1 tablespoon chopped fresh
  oregano *or* 1 teaspoon dried
  oregano
2 teaspoons raspberry vinegar
  (page 162) or cider vinegar
3oz/75g Feta cheese

1   Fry the onion and pepper gently in the olive oil for 10–15 minutes.

2   Add the oregano and raspberry or cider vinegar. Combine with the cooked pasta, crumble the Feta cheese on top and mix gently before serving.

One-pot Pasta

Although the most common method of cooking pasta is to boil it, it is equally successful when baked in a sauce in the oven.

SERVES 4

2 tablespoons olive oil
1 large onion, finely chopped
2 cloves garlic, crushed
6oz/175g mushrooms, quartered
2 carrots, grated
1 14oz/400g tin tomatoes, chopped *or* 1lb/450g fresh tomatoes, skinned and chopped
2–3 tablespoons tomato purée

1 teaspoon dried oregano
1 teaspoon dried basil
5fl oz/150ml water
4oz/110g Cheddar cheese, grated
12oz/350g wholemeal pasta (spirals or shells are ideal)
2 tablespoons grated Parmesan cheese
salt and freshly ground black pepper

1   Heat the oil in a large flameproof casserole, add the onion, garlic and mushrooms and cook over a medium heat for about 5 minutes. Add the carrots, tomatoes (if using tinned tomatoes add the juice as well), tomato purée, oregano and basil. Add the water, cover the pan and simmer gently for another 5 minutes. Remove from the heat and stir in the Cheddar cheese until it melts.

2   Mix the uncooked pasta into the sauce, adding extra water if necessary to ensure that the pasta is well coated and the sauce is fairly liquid. Sprinkle the top with Parmesan, cover and cook in the oven at 350°F/180°C/gas mark 4 for about 30 minutes, until the pasta is soft. Remove the lid for the last few minutes to brown the top.

Pasta alla Crema

A creamy pasta dish which is quick and easy to cook yet very special to eat.

SERVES 4

12oz/350g pasta shells
8oz/225g fresh or frozen peas
2oz/50g margarine or butter
1 onion, finely sliced
2 cloves garlic, crushed
2 medium carrots, coarsely grated
8 black olives, stoned and halved

5fl oz/150ml fromage frais, smetana or soured cream
a little milk
4oz/110g Gruyère cheese, grated
salt and freshly ground black pepper

1   Cook the pasta shells in boiling water until *al dente*. Drain and set aside.

2   Meanwhile, cook the peas in a little boiling water, drain and set aside.

3   Melt the margarine or butter in a pan over a medium heat, add the onion, garlic and carrots, cover and cook for about 10 minutes until soft and golden brown. Stir in the cooked peas, olives and fromage frais, smetana or soured cream. Add the cooked pasta and mix very gently over a low heat to coat the pasta well. If necessary, add a little milk if the sauce seems too thick.

4   Carefully stir in the cheese, season with salt and pepper and serve.

Hazelnut Pesto

Pesto is usually made with pine nuts and lots of fresh basil. Since it can be quite difficult to get hold of fresh basil, I've suggested here an 'alternative' pesto, which uses readily available ingredients.

SERVES 4

4oz/110g hazelnuts, finely
chopped
4 cloves garlic, crushed
4 tablespoons grated Parmesan
cheese
2 teaspoons dried oregano
3 tablespoons tomato purée
2 teaspoons concentrated
apple juice

5 tablespoons olive oil
1 teaspoon shoyu
3 tablespoons water
freshly ground black pepper
12oz/350g pasta (spirals, shells
or spaghetti)
extra Parmesan cheese for
serving

1   Mix together all the ingredients except the pasta in a heatproof bowl.

2   Cook the pasta in plenty of boiling water until *al dente*.

3   Meanwhile, warm the sauce very gently by placing the bowl over a small pan of water on top of the cooker. Bring the water to a gentle simmer and stir the sauce in the bowl as it warms through.

4   Drain the pasta and coat well with the sauce. Serve with extra Parmesan.

Spaghetti with Flageolet Bean and Mushroom Sauce

SERVES 4

4oz/110g dried flageolet beans
or 8oz/225g tinned beans
1 onion, finely chopped
6oz/175g mushrooms, roughly
chopped
2 tablespoons olive oil

9fl oz/275ml creamed tomatoes
or *passata*
2 bay leaves
1 teaspoon dried thyme
1½in/3.5cm stick cinnamon
10–12oz/275–350g spaghetti

1   If you are using dried beans, soak and cook them in the same way as for the chick peas on page 126.

2   Fry the onion and mushrooms gently in the olive oil for 10 minutes. Add the cooked beans, creamed tomatoes, bay leaves, thyme and cinnamon stick. Cover and simmer for 20–30 minutes.

3   Meanwhile, cook the spaghetti in plenty of boiling water until *al dente*. Drain and serve coated with the sauce.

Pasta with Cheese and Basil Sauce

A simple yet tasty supper or lunch dish. If you like basil but are unable to find the fresh leaves in the shops, it is worth growing it yourself – the flavour of fresh leaves is far superior to the dried version, and they make a great difference to salads and stews, and a delicious addition to sandwiches.

SERVES 4

12oz/350g pasta (shells or spirals are ideal)
2oz/50g margarine
1 onion, finely chopped
2oz/50g fine wholemeal flour
15fl oz/400ml milk
5fl oz/150ml water
1 clove garlic, crushed
2 tablespoons fresh basil, chopped *or* 2 teaspoons dried basil
4oz/110g Cheddar cheese, grated
2 tablespoons grated Parmesan cheese
salt and freshly ground black pepper

1   Cook the pasta in plenty of boiling water until *al dente*. Drain and set aside.

2   Meanwhile, prepare the sauce. Heat the margarine in a flame-proof casserole and cook the onion for 3–4 minutes. Stir in the flour and cook for a minute. Take off the heat and gradually add the milk and water, mixing well. Return to the heat and bring to the boil, stirring continuously. Simmer gently for 3–4 minutes to make a thick sauce. Remove from the heat.

3   Add the garlic, basil and Cheddar cheese and mix carefully until the cheese is melted. Add the cooked pasta, season with salt and pepper and mix well. Sprinkle with the Parmesan and place under a medium grill for 2–3 minutes to brown before serving.

Stir-fry

Stir-frying is one of the most energy-efficient methods of cooking, the idea being that you cook small pieces of food very quickly at a high temperature. The best pan to use is a wok – a shallow, wide-based pan, which, because of its large surface area, brings much of the food into contact with the heat source. If you don't have one of these then a heavy-based, large, cast-iron casserole will do as well, or try a large frying-pan.

Stir-frying is good for main courses: most of the cooking time is spent preparing the food, and very little time is needed for cooking. You can stir-fry almost anything – meat, fish, vegetables, and don't forget that you can add nuts, cooked beans, rice or other cereals, and even cubes of cheese, which, if added right at the end of the cooking, will just begin to melt and mix in nicely with the rest of the ingredients. Add spices at the beginning of the cooking if you like a hot or aromatic flavour, or sprinkle with dried or fresh herbs towards the end of the cooking. You can also sprinkle with flavoured oils, such as sesame oil and nut oils, and shoyu or lemon juice at the end to give subtle flavours; and if you are using meat or fish these can be flavoured and tenderised in advance by marinating them in shoyu, sherry, crushed garlic and finely chopped ginger root.

Here is a basic vegetable stir-fry recipe, to which you can add your own touches. Serve it with Chinese Egg Rice (page 88), pasta or jacket potatoes.

Basic Stir-fry

SERVES 4

2lb/900g mixed vegetables
(e.g. onions or shallots,
mushrooms, French beans,
tomatoes, parsnips, celery,
carrots, baby sweetcorn,
peppers, cauliflower, leeks,
cabbage, peas, etc.)

2 tablespoons sunflower oil
1 teaspoon cumin seeds
1 teaspoon coriander seeds
2 cloves garlic, chopped
2 tablespoons shoyu
1 tablespoon lemon juice or
apple juice

1   Prepare the vegetables by cutting or shredding into thin or small pieces. Arrange the vegetables according to how long they take to cook.

2   Heat the oil in a wok or pan over a medium heat, add the cumin and coriander seeds and the garlic and cook for 1 minute. Turn the heat up high and add the vegetables, one at a time, starting with the ones that take the longest to cook, e.g. onion, cauliflower, carrot, and leaving vegetables like mushrooms, cabbage and peas until the end. Stir the vegetables frequently to ensure even cooking. The whole process should take about 10 minutes. Sprinkle over the shoyu and lemon juice or apple juice before serving.

Sweet and Sour Stir-fry

You can either serve the stir-fry 'dry' as above, or add a little liquid at the end of the cooking so that the vegetables are coated in a delicious sauce. Instead of sprinkling on the shoyu and lemon juice, stir in this sauce over the heat as the stir-fry finishes cooking, and let the sauce thicken before serving.

½ pint/275ml water	2 tablespoons tomato purée
2 tablespoons arrowroot	1 tablespoon shoyu
1 tablespoon concentrated apple juice	1 tablespoon cider vinegar

1   Mix a little of the water with the arrowroot to make a thick paste. Stir in the rest of the water and then add the apple juice, tomato purée, shoyu and cider vinegar.

2   Pour over the vegetables in the pan and continue to cook for 2–3 minutes, stirring continuously, until the sauce thickens and the vegetables are coated in the sauce.

Spinach Gnocchi

An impressive yet simple dish to make, particularly good if you have lots of spinach in the garden. Serve these little gnocchi with a simple tomato or mushroom sauce (pages 106–7) and a good green salad.

SERVES 4

1½lb/700g spinach	2oz/50g flour
4oz/110g butter or margarine	2oz/50g grated Parmesan
8oz/225g curd cheese	cheese
2oz/50g Cheddar cheese, grated	salt and freshly ground black pepper
2 eggs, beaten	

1   Cook the spinach in a large pan over a moderate heat until tender – you don't need to use any liquid as the spinach loses water very quickly once it starts to cook. Drain and chop finely.

2   Melt 2oz/50g of the butter or margarine in the same pan and add the cooked spinach and curd and Cheddar cheeses. Mix well over the heat for 2 minutes.

3   Remove from the heat and add the eggs, flour and half of the Parmesan. Season with a little salt and pepper and set aside until cold.

4   On a floured board form little sausage shapes out of the spinach mixture and coat very lightly in flour. Drop a few gnocchi at a time into a large pan of boiling water, and simmer very gently for 2–3 minutes until cooked. Drain and repeat until all the gnocchi are cooked.

5   Place in a well-buttered ovenproof dish. Melt the remaining butter, pour over and then sprinkle with the rest of the Parmesan. Grill under medium heat until brown and bubbling.

Spicy Onion Fritters

Vegetable fritters can be made with many different types of vegetable and are especially simple if you use a batter made with chick pea (gram) flour. No eggs or milk are needed – gram flour mixed with water makes a thick coating batter which puffs up beautifully when fried. This type of batter forms the basis for the Indian-style fritters, or onion bahjiis, below, but try it with other vegetables, too, such as courgettes, mushrooms, cauliflower and peppers. These fritters can be served as part of a main course, as a first course or even as a side dish.

MAKES 8 BAHJIIS OR FRITTERS

3oz/75g chick pea (gram) flour
4fl oz/100ml water
1 teaspoon ground cumin
seeds
1 teaspoon ground coriander
seeds
a pinch of chilli powder

2 medium onions, finely
shredded
3 cloves garlic, crushed
salt and freshly ground black
pepper
sunflower oil for frying
lemon quarters to serve

1   Put the flour in a bowl and gradually incorporate the water to form a thick, smooth batter.

2   Add the ground cumin and coriander seeds, chilli powder, salt and pepper. Mix in the onions and garlic.

3   Heat about ¾in/2cm oil in a deep frying-pan over a medium heat. Drop spoonfuls of the batter into the fat and cook until brown underneath. Turn and brown the other side. Do not allow the fritters to brown too quickly or the inside will remain uncooked. Drain and serve immediately with lemon quarters.

Proper Pizza

Real pizzas are easy to make and so much better than shop-bought ones. For the best results you need a very hot oven, so do make use of the oven as it is heating up and cooling down – cook some jacket potatoes in the bottom, putting them in as you turn the oven on and finishing their cooking as the oven cools down afterwards. Instructions are also given for a more energy-efficient method of cooking under the grill if you do not wish to use your oven.

SERVES 4

8oz/225g unbleached strong white bread flour
1 teaspoon salt
1 teaspoon easy-mix instant dried yeast
2 tablespoons olive oil
4fl oz/100ml warm water
1 onion, finely chopped
2 cloves garlic, crushed
1lb/450g ripe tomatoes, chopped *or* 1 14oz/400g tin chopped tomatoes

2 tablespoons chopped fresh basil *or* 2 teaspoons dried basil
freshly ground black pepper
4oz/110g Mozzarella cheese, roughly grated
olives, capers, rings of green pepper for garnish

1 Mix the flour, salt and dried yeast in a bowl. Combine 1 tablespoon of the oil with the water and then pour into the flour mixture. Using a knife, draw together into a rough dough and turn out onto a floured surface. Knead the dough for 5–10 minutes until it is smooth and elastic. Return to the bowl, cover with a damp tea towel and leave to rise in a warm place for 1 hour.

2 Meanwhile, heat the remaining oil in a pan and add the onion and garlic. Cook for 5 minutes over a medium heat and then add the tomatoes, herbs and black pepper. Cook for a further 5 minutes, turning the heat up high to reduce the liquid if the mixture seems very moist. Remove from the heat and allow to cool a little.

3   Heat the oven to 475°F/240°C/gas mark 9. Turn out the dough and knead lightly before rolling out into a circle 10–12in/25–30.5cm in diameter. Place on a greased baking tray, cover with the tomato mixture and then the cheese. Add a garnish of olives, capers and pepper rings. Bake in the top of the oven for 10–15 minutes until brown.

Note   If this is the only cooking you are doing in the oven, it may be more energy-efficient to cook your pizza under the grill. The result will be good, though not quite so authentic as the oven-cooked version.

Grease an oblong baking tray the same size as the grill pan of your cooker. Turn out the dough and knead lightly before rolling out thinly to fit the baking tray. The rolled-out dough must be quite thin for this method of cooking, so depending on the size of your tray there may be enough dough to make two pizzas. Put the tray of pizza base under a medium grill for 5–10 minutes to cook lightly, but do not allow it to become too brown. Remove from under the grill and cover with the tomato mixture, cheese and garnishes, return under the grill and cook for a further 5–10 minutes, again making sure that it does not burn.

Speciality Rice

A good recipe for using any vegetables you have in store. I have suggested some here but you can substitute whatever you like. Potatoes would need to be par-boiled first. You could also use cooked rice that you have left from the previous day, but do remember that cooked rice must be kept in the fridge and should be used within 24 hours.

SERVES 4

12oz/350g long-grain brown rice *or* 1½lb/700g cooked rice

1½ pints/900ml water

2 tablespoons olive oil

1 red onion, finely chopped

3 cloves garlic, chopped

2 teaspoons mild curry powder (look for a fragrant variety)

1 small parsnip, finely sliced

4 courgettes, sliced

6 large mushrooms, cut into chunks

5 tomatoes, chopped

¼ white cabbage, shredded

2oz/50g Cheddar cheese, cubed

salt or shoyu and freshly ground black pepper

1   Bring the water to the boil, wash the rice, and add to the water. Cover and then simmer gently for 25–30 minutes, until the rice is cooked and the water has been absorbed.

2   Heat the oil in a large, heavy pan over a moderate heat and add the onion, garlic and curry powder. Cook gently for 5 minutes.

3   Add the rest of the vegetables and continue cooking for a further 10 minutes, stirring occasionally to prevent sticking.

4   Add the cooked rice and cook for another 10 minutes. Remove from the heat, add the cheese cubes, cover the pan and leave to stand for a minute or two to allow the cheese to melt. Season with a little salt and pepper, or shoyu if you prefer, and serve.

Choice Bulgar

Bulgar wheat (sometimes known as cracked wheat) is a good standby for the green cook. It is cooked by simply soaking in boiling water for about 10 minutes, after which the fluffed-up grain can be used as a basis for salads, to accompany casseroles or stews instead of rice, or as a main course dish similar to a pilaff. Here is my special recipe for bulgar 'pilaff'.

SERVES 4

12oz/350g bulgar wheat
1 teaspoon salt
1 teaspoon dried mint
1 teaspoon dried basil
2 tablespoons olive oil
2 teaspoons cider vinegar
1 teaspoon concentrated apple juice
1 mild red onion *or* 3 spring onions, very finely chopped
2oz/50g cashew nuts, toasted
2oz/50g Feta cheese, goats' cheese or Cheddar cheese, diced

1oz/25g raisins, soaked in hot water for 10 minutes and drained
6 small tomatoes, quartered
1 stick celery, chopped
2 small eating apples, diced
a large handful of chopped fresh parsley
freshly ground black pepper
2 teaspoons walnut or hazelnut oil (optional)

1   Put the bulgar wheat, salt, mint and basil in a large bowl. Cover with boiling water, making sure that the water is about ½in/1cm above the level of the wheat. Leave to soak for about 10 minutes, stirring once or twice. At the end of this time all the water should be absorbed. If not, drain off any excess.

2   Add the olive oil, cider vinegar and concentrated apple juice to the warm bulgar and mix well.

3   Add the remaining ingredients, mixing carefully together. Stir in the walnut or hazelnut oil just before serving to make the pilaff extra smooth and tasty.

Crisp-fried Goats' Cheese

This simple idea originates from France. Though you can now buy the cheese ready-prepared for cooking, it is very easy to do this yourself at home. Serve as a snack or as a light summery main course with a selection of salads.

SERVES 4

4oz/110g wholemeal
   breadcrumbs
1 clove garlic, crushed
1 teaspoon dried thyme
2 tablespoons olive oil

4 individual goats' cheeses *or* 8
   thick slices from a large
   cheese
sunflower oil for frying

1   Mix together the breadcrumbs, garlic, thyme and olive oil. Thickly coat the individual cheeses or slices with the breadcrumb mixture, pressing it well into the surface of the cheese.

2   Fry the cheeses gently in the sunflower oil for 5–10 minutes, turning until brown on all sides. Serve immediately.

Green Stuffed Peppers

These stuffed peppers need little cooking and, unlike some vegetables, are easy to stuff. Grilling the peppers before stuffing them makes them sweet and juicy.

SERVES 4

1 quantity of prepared Choice
   Bulgar (see page 121), warmed
2 very large or 4 small red or
   green peppers

2oz/50g Cheddar
   cheese, grated

1   Cut the peppers in half lengthwise, remove the seeds and place cut side down under a medium grill. Grill until the skin becomes crisp and blackened, turning the peppers to ensure that all the skin cooks. Cool and then peel off the blackened skin. Put the pepper halves cut side up on an ovenproof serving dish.

2   Fill the peppers with the Choice Bulgar, sprinkle the grated cheese on top and then put back under the grill for 1–2 minutes to melt the cheese. Serve immediately.

Flat Bread

This lovely idea, perfect for a picnic, originates from Southern France. Its name derives from the 'flattening' stage, during which the bread absorbs the wonderful juices of the oil, olives and tomatoes and becomes succulent and pink.

SERVES 4

1 baguette or French loaf	1 clove garlic, crushed
8 black olives, stoned and finely chopped	4 tablespoons olive oil
	4 large tomatoes, sliced
2 tablespoons chopped fresh parsley	1 red pepper, sliced

1   Slit the loaf lengthwise.

2   Mash the olives, parsley and garlic together with the olive oil, and spread on both cut sides of the loaf.

3   Lay slices of tomatoes and pepper along the length of the loaf and sandwich both halves together. Tie with string and place under a bread board with a heavy weight on top. Leave for 1 hour before untying and serving in slices.

Mushroom and Almond Goulash

As with many of these recipes, you can either cook this on top of the cooker or in the oven, depending on what else you are cooking at the time. Don't forget that you could cook a pot of 'boiled' rice alongside this dish in the oven, ensuring not only energy efficiency but also the perfect accompaniment to this creamy, slightly spicy casserole.

SERVES 4

2 tablespoons sunflower oil
2oz/50g whole almonds
1 onion, finely sliced
2 cloves garlic, chopped
1½ tablespoons paprika
1 teaspoon caraway seeds
1 teaspoon dried thyme
8oz/225g mushrooms, quartered

8oz/225g tomatoes, chopped
4 medium potatoes, diced
1 tablespoon tomato purée
7fl oz/200ml water
salt and freshly ground black pepper
5fl oz/150ml soured cream or smetana

1   Heat the oil in a large pan or flameproof casserole over a medium heat. Add the almonds and toast them in the oil for 2–3 minutes.

2   Add the onion, garlic, paprika, caraway seeds and thyme and cook for another 2–3 minutes.

3   Add the mushrooms, tomatoes, potatoes, tomato purée and water. Bring to the boil, cover and cook gently, either in the oven at 350°F/180°C/gas mark 4 for 30–40 minutes or on top of the cooker for 25–30 minutes. Remove the lid during the last 10 minutes of cooking to allow the sauce to reduce if necessary.

4   Remove from the heat, season with salt and pepper and gently mix in half the soured cream or smetana, swirling in an extra spoonful to each dish of goulash before serving.

Aubergine and Mozzarella Pie

Serve with plain rice or pasta.

SERVES 4

2 tablespoons olive oil
1 onion, finely chopped
4 cloves garlic, chopped
1lb/450g tomatoes, chopped
    or 1 14oz/400g tin tomatoes
8oz/225g small mushrooms,
    halved
2 teaspoons dried oregano
1 tablespoon tomato purée

4fl oz/100ml water or juice
    from tinned tomatoes
2 small aubergines, thinly
    sliced
4oz/110g Mozzarella, thinly
    sliced
salt and freshly ground black
    pepper

1   Heat the oil in a pan, add the onion and garlic and cook over a medium heat for 4–5 minutes.

2   Add the tomatoes (if you are using tinned tomatoes, drain and reserve the juice) and the mushrooms and cook for a further 5 minutes.

3   Add the oregano, tomato purée and water or tomato juice, bring to the boil and simmer gently for 5 minutes. Season with salt and pepper.

4   Meanwhile, preheat the oven to 375°F/190°C/gas mark 5. Arrange the aubergine slices on a baking tray, brush them with a little oil and put in the oven for 8–10 minutes as it is heating up. Remove from the oven.

5   Spoon half of the tomato sauce into an ovenproof dish. Cover with half the aubergine slices and then with half the cheese slices. Add the remaining sauce, the remaining aubergine and then finish with the remaining cheese. Cover the casserole and cook in the preheated oven for 35–40 minutes, removing the lid for the last 10 minutes to brown the cheese.

Chick Pea Curry

Serve this Indian-style dish with Lemon Rice (page 92) for a complete meal. If you do not have a pressure cooker to speed up cooking the chick peas or if you are unable to cook them in advance in the oven with other dishes to save energy, you could use tinned chick peas.

SERVES 4

8oz/225g uncooked chick peas
or 1 15oz/425g tin chick
peas, drained

2 tablespoons sunflower oil
1 large onion, finely chopped
2 cloves garlic, crushed

Spices

2 tablespoons mild curry
powder
or
1 teaspoon ground cumin
seeds

2 teaspoons ground coriander
seeds
1 teaspoon turmeric
¼ teaspoon chilli powder
1 teaspoon garam masala

1½lb/700g potatoes, diced
4oz/110g red split lentils
1¼pints/700ml water

salt or shoyu and freshly
ground black pepper

1   If you are using uncooked chick peas, soak them overnight in a bowl of cold water or for 1 hour in boiling water. Drain, cover with fresh water, bring to the boil, cover the pan and boil fast for 10 minutes. Reduce the heat and simmer gently for 30–40 minutes until the chick peas are just cooked. (This can also be done in a moderate oven. Alternatively, using a pressure cooker will cut the cooking time by up to two-thirds.) Drain the cooked chick peas.

2   Heat the oil in a large flameproof casserole and add the onion and garlic. Mix in the curry powder or the mixture of individual spices, and cook gently for 10 minutes.

3   Add the cooked or tinned chick peas, the potatoes, lentils and the water. Bring to the boil, cover and simmer gently for 30–40 minutes, until the potatoes and lentils are cooked. Again, this can be done in the oven. Season well with salt or shoyu and pepper before serving.

Leek and Mushroom Ring

A simple, attractive dish – serve with a bright side dish, such as Carrots and Chilli (page 79) or French Peas (page 86).

SERVES 4

1½lb/700g potatoes, peeled	1½ tablespoons wholemeal flour
2½oz/60g margarine or butter	
2 tablespoons natural yoghurt	1½ teaspoons dried thyme
4 tablespoons chopped fresh parsley	¼ teaspoon cayenne pepper
	2 teaspoons paprika
8oz/225g small leeks, chopped	½ pint/275ml milk
8oz/225g small mushrooms, halved	1 tablespoon shoyu

1   Cook the potatoes in boiling water. Drain and mash, adding 1oz/25g of the margarine or butter. Mix in the yoghurt and parsley and arrange in a ring around the edge of a large, shallow ovenproof dish. Keep warm.

2   Melt the remaining margarine or butter in a pan, add the leeks and mushrooms and cook over a medium heat for 5–8 minutes. Sprinkle over the flour, thyme, cayenne pepper and paprika and mix well. Remove from the heat and add the milk. Return to the heat and simmer gently until the sauce thickens. Add the shoyu.

3   Pour the leek and mushroom mixture into the centre of the potato ring and warm through, either in a 375°F/190°C/gas mark 5 oven or under a medium grill.

Briam

This dish, a Greek recipe of vegetables baked with cheese, is quickly prepared before being left to cook in the oven. I have used Parmesan, which is readily available in this country, instead of the authentic Greek cheese, graviera. For the best flavour the olive oil should be extra-virgin oil from Greece.

SERVES 4

4–5 medium potatoes
3 medium courgettes
4–5 large, juicy tomatoes or 1 14oz/400g tin tomatoes
6 cloves garlic
2oz/50g Feta cheese, crumbled

5fl oz/150ml water or juice from tinned tomatoes
2–3fl oz/50–75ml olive oil
2 tablespoons grated Parmesan cheese
salt and freshly ground black pepper

1   Slice the potatoes, courgettes and tomatoes thinly. If using tinned tomatoes, drain them, reserving the juice, and then chop finely. Chop the garlic finely.

2   Brush the inside of a large baking dish with a little of the olive oil and then layer the potatoes, courgettes, tomatoes and garlic with the crumbled Feta cheese in the dish. Season well with pepper and salt. Pour over the water, or the reserved tomato juice with a little water, together with the olive oil. Sprinkle the top with the Parmesan.

3   Cover the dish and bake in the oven at 350°F/180°C/gas mark 4 for 1 hour, uncovering the dish for the last 15 minutes. Check during the cooking and add a little extra water if necessary.

Mushroom Sandwich

This recipe is perfect for using large field mushrooms if you are lucky enough to come across them. It makes a simple main course that would go well with creamy mashed potatoes and a moist vegetable accompaniment such as French Peas (page 86) or Spanish Courgettes (page 82), both of which could be cooked in the oven alongside the mushrooms.

SERVES 4

8 large, flat mushrooms
2 tablespoons olive oil
1 large onion, chopped
8oz/225g wholemeal
   breadcrumbs

4oz/110g walnuts, ground or
   very finely chopped
2 teaspoons dried oregano
4 tablespoons tomato purée
a little water

1   Remove the stalks from the mushrooms and chop the stalks finely, leaving the mushroom cups whole.

2   Heat the oil in a pan and fry the onion and mushroom stalks over a moderate heat for 5–10 minutes. Remove from the heat.

3   Add the breadcrumbs, walnuts, oregano and tomato purée to the pan, and mix well. Add enough water to make a mixture that is not too dry and will hold together.

4   Lightly oil a small ovenproof casserole. Divide the nut mixture into four and use it to sandwich together the mushroom cups in pairs. Put the mushroom sandwiches into the casserole, cover and bake in the oven at 400°F/200°C/gas mark 6 for 15–20 minutes.

Barbecue Burgers

These little hazelnut burgers are a popular choice for all types of meal, not least a barbecue, in which case they can be charcoal grilled very successfully. They are also an excellent way of using up leftover bread.

MAKES 8 SMALL BURGERS

4oz/110g hazelnuts
4oz/110g wholemeal breadcrumbs
1 tablespoon olive oil
1 onion, finely chopped
1 carrot, finely grated
1 eating apple, grated
2oz/50g mushrooms, finely chopped
1 tablespoon chopped fresh thyme *or* 1 teaspoon dried thyme

1 tablespoon chopped fresh sage *or* 1 teaspoon dried sage
1 tablespoon shoyu
1 tablespoon tomato purée dissolved in 5fl oz/150ml water
1 egg, beaten
a few tablespoons of breadcrumbs or porridge oats
sunflower oil for frying

1   Chop the hazelnuts as finely as possible, or roughly grind them in a grinder when making the breadcrumbs. Mix with the breadcrumbs in a large bowl.

2   Put the olive oil into a pan over a medium heat and add the onion, carrot, apple and mushrooms. Cook gently for 10 minutes until the vegetables begin to brown.

3   Add the cooked vegetables to the nuts and breadcrumbs with the thyme and sage, mixing well. Stir in the shoyu and the tomato purée and water. Mix together and then form into eight burger shapes. Dip each burger into the egg and coat with breadcrumbs or porridge oats.

4   Heat the sunflower oil in a large frying-pan over a medium heat. Cook the burgers carefully for 5–8 minutes on each side, making sure they do not burn. Alternatively, grill over a barbecue; brush lightly with oil and turn the burgers carefully during cooking.

FISH AND MEAT

These dishes use either good quality meat or fresh fish; since meat in particular is an expensive form of protein always serve plenty of vegetables or salads alongside.

If you live near the coast then you may be able to buy your fish direct from the fisherman and this is by far the best way. It is very fresh, usually excellent quality and very economical. Don't forget that if you are able to buy fish in this way you can make good use of your freezer. If you buy your fish from a fishmonger, make sure that it is fresh and bright looking. Some large supermarkets are beginning to have excellent fish counters, although they tend to be a little more expensive.

It is more difficult to buy good meat on a day-to-day basis, unless you have a good local butcher or farm selling real, organic free-range meat (see page 12). Apart from the fact that the flavour and quality of 'real' meat is so superior, from a green point of view most commercially produced meat is unacceptable. This may mean that you decide to limit your intake of meat to special occasions when you can afford to have good quality meat that you can really enjoy. Many organic meat producers offer a bulk order postal service so that you can fill your freezer easily. Alternatively, you could seek out sources of wild game. The recipes in this book include ideas for game, chicken, and lamb, all of which are easiest to obtain as 'real' meat. When you do cook meat do so with care – good quality real meat often only needs the simplest cooking for the best results.

Fish Soup

If you are able to buy fish direct from fishermen it is always cheaper than from any shop and is almost certain to be fresher, too. If you have a freezer, buy a quantity of fish to make your journey worthwhile. Whiting is the fish recommended for this dish, but almost any white fish will do. The smoked haddock adds a bite to the flavour – look for genuine oak-smoked haddock, and check that it is undyed.

SERVES 4

1½lb/700g whiting, ling, monkfish or cod cut into 1oz/25g chunks
4oz/110g smoked haddock cut into 1oz/25g chunks
2oz/50g butter
1 medium onion, chopped
2 cloves garlic, finely chopped
6oz/175g button mushrooms, half finely sliced, the rest cut in half

6 small tomatoes, chopped
4 medium potatoes, finely sliced
2 tablespoons tomato purée
1½ pints/900ml water
2 bay leaves
2 teaspoons dried marjoram

1   Melt the butter in a heavy flameproof casserole, and fry the onion, garlic and sliced mushrooms for 10 minutes.

2   Add the tomatoes and, after 2 minutes, the potatoes, mushroom halves, and pieces of fish.

3   Mix the tomato purée with the water and pour it into the casserole, adding the bay leaves and marjoram. Cover and place in the oven at 375°F/190°C/gas mark 5 for 45 minutes to 1 hour, until the potatoes are cooked through.

Fried Sardines with Tzatziki

In Britain, fresh sardines tend to be rather large, so ask the fishmonger for small ones or choose large whitebait instead. Serve each portion with a generous half of lemon.

SERVES 4

1lb/450g small, fresh sardines
4oz/110g wholemeal flour
olive oil for frying

salt and freshly ground black
  pepper
2 lemons for serving

1   Wipe the fish and remove any large scales (this will only be necessary if you are using larger sardines). Season the flour with salt and pepper, and coat the fish lightly with the flour.

2   Heat the oil in a frying-pan and fry the fish over a medium heat for 5–10 minutes, gently turning until crisp and brown. Serve immediately with the lemon.

Tzatziki

Perfect for serving with fried sardines, this easy dip has many other uses. Try it as a salad dressing, as a sauce for cooked rice or pasta, or simply scoop it up with chunks of bread as they do in Greece where this dish originates.

SERVES 4

1 medium cucumber
½ pint/275ml Greek-style
  yoghurt

4 cloves garlic, crushed
a squeeze of lemon juice
salt

1   Peel the cucumber, or leave the skin on if you prefer. Coarsely grate the cucumber into a bowl, pouring off the excess juice.

2   Add the yoghurt to the bowl with the crushed garlic and a little lemon juice to taste. Season lightly with salt and chill until serving.

Grilled Flatfish with Tomato Sauce

Dabs are an inexpensive flatfish – far cheaper than sole or plaice. Although less popular, they have a good flavour and cooked by this simple method are a delight. Any flatfish can be cooked in this way.

SERVES 4

4 8oz/225g dabs, sole or plaice, cleaned
2 tablespoons olive oil

the juice of 1 lemon
freshly ground black pepper

Tomato sauce

3 tablespoons margarine
2 tablespoons wholemeal flour
12oz/350g tomatoes, chopped
   or 1 14oz/400g tin chopped
   tomatoes

4 cloves garlic, chopped
1 tablespoon concentrated
   apple juice
1 satsuma *or* 1 small sweet
   orange in segments

1   First make the sauce. In a small heavy pan soften the margarine over a medium heat, add the flour and stir for a few minutes. Pour in the tomatoes and continue stirring. Add the garlic, apple juice and satsuma or orange segments. Simmer for 5 minutes and keep warm.

2   Brush both sides of the fish with the olive oil and sprinkle with black pepper. Place bottom (pale) sides up under a hot grill for 7 minutes. Remove from the grill, turn the fish over and squeeze the lemon juice onto the darker sides of the fish. Grill this side for 5 minutes.

Herrings Grilled with Mustard

Herrings are a real pleasure to eat – they are also nutritious, cheap and a very traditional British fish. They are at their best from late summer to mid-autumn, although it is possible to buy them all the year round. They are a versatile fish, and this simple recipe is a good one to introduce you to the pleasures of herring-eating.

SERVES 4

4 medium or large herrings	2 tablespoons wholegrain
2 tablespoons olive oil	mustard

1   If you are buying your herring from a fishmonger ask him to clean and bone your fish. If your fish have come direct from the fisherman, you will need to prepare them yourself. Scrape off any scales with the back of a knife, working from tail to head. Cut off the head and tail, and remove the fins – there are two on the underside, two near the head end, two towards the tail, one along the back.

Slit along the belly and remove innards and roe (if you like roe then it can be grilled along with the fish).

To remove the backbone, open the fish and lay it belly down, and run your knuckles along the back firmly a few times. This loosens the backbone, which you can easily pull off when you turn the fish over. Wash the fish under the cold tap and dry them.

2   Brush the skin side of the fish with the olive oil, place in a grill pan under a high heat for 5–8 minutes, according to the thickness of the fish.

3   Turn the fish over, spread the mustard not too thickly onto the flesh and return to the grill for a further 4–6 minutes.

Mackerel with Shallots and Tomatoes

Buy your mackerel ideally direct from fishermen or from a reputable fishmonger – never buy mackerel with sunken eyes or a generally dull look. Apart from tasting good, recent research has shown that mackerel is a nutritious and healthy food for people with potential circulatory problems. Grey mullet can also be used in this recipe. Serve with white or wholemeal pasta, which soaks up the juices and does not interfere with the subtle flavours.

SERVES 4

4 fresh mackerel, cleaned and trimmed, heads and tails removed
1oz/25g butter or margarine
8oz/225g small shallots or pickling onions, quartered
2 tablespoons fresh dill, finely chopped *or* 1 teaspoon dried dill

1lb/450g tomatoes, the smallest you can find, halved
1 glass dry white wine or apple juice
1 tablespoon olive oil
freshly ground black pepper

1   Heat the butter in a flameproof baking dish or oval casserole and, over a medium heat, cook the shallots or pickling onions until soft. Remove from the heat and stir in 1 tablespoon of the fresh dill or all of the dried dill and two good pinches of pepper.

2   Lay the mackerel, open side down, on the shallots, with any soft roes in between, and surround with the tomato halves. Pour the white wine or apple juice over the fish and brush them with the olive oil.

3   Bake uncovered in the oven at 350°F/180°C/gas mark 4, until the skin of the fish is brown and blistered and the flesh is ready to fall from the bone. This takes about 45 minutes, depending on the size of the fish. You may need to add a little extra liquid during the cooking. Sprinkle with the remaining fresh dill before serving.

Red Mullet

Red mullet has a subtle flavour; it is not always available, but some supermarkets stock it and it is worth asking for it at your local fishmonger. Make a special friend of your fishmonger, and he will not only point out to you anything 'unusual' he has available but will probably let you have all kinds of special bits and pieces at a very low price, such as fish heads for a cheap soup.

SERVES 4

1lb 4oz/550g red mullet, cleaned
2 medium red peppers, sliced
8oz/225g mushrooms, sliced

4oz/110g very small onions (pickling onions), left whole
1 teaspoon cornflour, mixed with 4 tablespoons water

Marinade

juice of half a lemon
8 tablespoons olive oil
3 cloves garlic, crushed
5 fresh sage leaves, finely chopped *or* 1 teaspoon dried sage

10 marjoram leaves, finely chopped *or* 2 teaspoons dried marjoram
5fl oz/150ml vegetable stock or water
freshly ground black pepper

1   If you decide to clean the fish yourself, remove fins and eyes, scrape off scales with the back of a knife – working from tail to head – gut, wash and wipe the fish.

2   Mix together the marinade ingredients, lay your fish in an ovenproof casserole and pour over the marinade. Leave for 1½ hours, turning the fish over after 45 minutes.

3   Take out the fish and add the peppers, mushrooms and onions to the marinade, and then lay the fish stomach-side down on the vegetables. Cover and bake in the oven at 350°F/180°C/gas mark 4 for 1 hour. Remove from the oven and stir the cornflour mixture into the juices. Return to the oven for a further 10 minutes.

When you come to serve the fish the flesh will easily fall away from the bones.

Fish Cakes

Coley is a cheap fish to buy, possibly on account of its grey colour when uncooked. However, it has a fine flavour and is perfect for fish cakes. These fish cakes are quite substantial; serve with a finely shredded Savoy or winter cabbage cooked for 5 minutes in 2 tablespoons butter and 2 tablespoons water. They are also excellent with fried parsley (see below).

SERVES 4

1lb/450g coley
2 bay leaves
5fl oz/150ml water
1½lb/700g potatoes, scrubbed
1oz/25g butter
1 medium onion, chopped to a pulp

a large handful of parsley, very finely chopped
4 tablespoons wholemeal flour
3 tablespoons olive oil
freshly ground black pepper

1   Put the coley and bay leaves in a small ovenproof casserole, add the water, cover and bake in the oven at 350°F/180°C/gas mark 4 for 30 minutes. Remove from the oven and discard any skin and bones. Break up the fish into small pieces.

2   Meanwhile, boil the potatoes, then drain and mash them with the butter. Stir in the onion and parsley and then the coley, mixing it in carefully with a fork.

3   Form the mixture into eight fish cakes and roll them in the flour seasoned with the black pepper.

4   Heat the olive oil in a frying-pan and fry the fish cakes for 5–8 minutes on each side, until they are well browned.

Fried Parsley

> a handful of parsley
> 1 tablespoon margarine or
>   olive oil

Heat the margarine or olive oil in a frying-pan. Fry the parsley for a few minutes, stirring occasionally, until the leaves are crisp and the stalks succulent.

Crab and Raspberries

Crab is a great delicacy and so are raspberries. You should be able to buy dressed crab from good fishmongers – do use the crab the day you buy it. It is possible and fun to pick your own raspberries at many fruit-farms. This is a light dish for lunchtime or to start the main meal of the day, and is best eaten with lightly buttered brown bread, toast or rice crackers.

SERVES 4

> 8oz/225g crab meat from 1
>   very large or 2 medium
>   dressed crabs
> 4oz/110g raspberries, washed
>
> 2 tablespoons fresh parsley,
>   finely chopped
> salt and freshly ground black
>   pepper

Mix all the ingredients together well with a fork until quite smooth. Chill for 20 minutes and serve.

Pigeons with Peas and Blackberries

Pigeons are very good in late summer, after they have been 'gleaning' the stubbles and are fat from their cropfuls of corn. It is better to buy pigeons ready plucked, as it is then possible to see that the birds have not been badly shot. If you are given pigeons still in feather, ask to be shown how to pluck and draw the birds. The principle is the same for all game birds and poultry, so it is a useful skill to acquire.

SERVES 4

2 large or 4 small pigeons
2 tablespoons olive oil
1 medium onion, finely
    chopped
1lb/450g fresh shelled peas
8oz/225g ripe blackberries,
    well washed

1 tablespoon finely chopped
    fresh mint or 1 teaspoon
    dried mint
5fl oz/150ml dry white wine,
    dry cider or apple juice
salt and freshly ground black
    pepper

1   Heat 1 tablespoon of the olive oil in a frying-pan and brown the onion. Transfer to an ovenproof casserole large enough to fit the pigeons fairly snugly, and add half the peas and blackberries and a little salt and pepper with the mint.

2   Brown the pigeons in the remaining oil and place them breast down in the casserole. Pack the rest of the peas and blackberries in between the pigeons and pour on the wine, cider or apple juice.

3   Cook covered in the oven at 425°F/220°C/gas mark 7 for 20 minutes. Lower the heat to 325°F/170°C/gas mark 3 and cook for a further 2 hours. Add a small amount of water during the cooking time if necessary.

4   Remove the pigeons, carve and keep hot. Mash the peas and blackberries into a sauce, and reduce the sauce carefully over a high heat if it is too liquid. Serve with pasta or boiled potatoes, pouring on the sauce immediately before serving.

Pork Stir-fry

Stir-frying is a quick way of producing a delicious meal, although the preparation takes a little time and care. It is important to use the finest cuts for cooking by this method. If you like your stir-fry to have a moist texture, use tomatoes, if not, simply leave them out. Serve with plain boiled rice, white or brown.

SERVES 4

12oz/350g pork escalope or tenderloin, cut into very thin slices and then thin strips
2 tablespoons sunflower oil
1 clove garlic, crushed
2 sticks celery, finely sliced
2 small green peppers, finely sliced
4oz/110g button mushrooms, sliced
1 hard dessert apple, peeled, cored and chopped

8oz/225g tomatoes, roughly chopped
3 spring onions, finely chopped
1 tablespoon shoyu
1 tablespoon cider vinegar
1 tablespoon concentrated apple juice
salt and freshly ground black pepper

1   Heat the oil and garlic in a wok or heavy, wide-based casserole over a high heat. Add the pork and fry, stirring constantly, for 3–4 minutes.

2   Throw in the celery, peppers, mushrooms and apple and then the tomatoes if you are using them. Continue stirring and after 1 minute or so add the spring onions, shoyu, vinegar, concentrated apple juice and salt and pepper to taste. Stir for one more minute and serve.

Wild Rabbit

Wild rabbit is succulent, with a distinctive flavour. It is also low in cholesterol-forming adipose fat. In a city or town it may be possible to locate a game-dealer where wild rabbit will be on sale. In the country look out for wild rabbits at local weekly auctions that may sell game, or ask your local butcher. If you buy a rabbit that has not been skinned, check that it has been gutted; this should have been done as soon as possible after the rabbit was killed. Rabbits that have been netted often sell for more than those which have been shot, since they will be undamaged and almost certain not to contain shot. Unlike most other game, rabbit should be eaten as soon after killing as possible.

SERVES 4

1 rabbit, jointed as described below
2oz/50g wholemeal flour
2 tablespoons olive oil
1 large onion, chopped
2 garlic cloves, crushed
3 carrots, sliced
6oz/175g small button mushrooms
1 teaspoon dried thyme
1 teaspoon dried marjoram

5fl oz/150ml orange juice
1 liqueur glass calvados or brandy
1 tablespoon wholegrain mustard
1 tablespoon crab apple or blackcurrant jelly
3 tablespoons chopped fresh parsley
salt and freshly ground black pepper

1   Joint the rabbit into five pieces: two hind legs, the back cut in two and the front legs and ribcage as one piece. Season the flour with salt and pepper, and coat the rabbit pieces with the flour.

2   Heat the olive oil in a heavy flameproof casserole and brown the rabbit pieces on all sides for 10 minutes. Add the onion, garlic, carrots and mushrooms, and cook for a further 10 minutes. Add the remaining ingredients, apart from the parsley, and mix well.

3   Cover the casserole and cook in the oven at 300°F/150°C/gas mark 2, for 1½–2 hours. An older rabbit will take longer to cook. Sprinkle with the chopped parsley as you serve the rabbit.

Braised Rabbit

Serve this rabbit stew with simple boiled brown rice.

SERVES 4

1 wild rabbit, jointed as
   described below
½ teaspoon paprika
1 tablespoon olive oil
4 sticks celery, each sliced into
   two lengthways
4 small leeks, chopped
4 small carrots, chopped
2 bay leaves
1 tablespoon fresh rosemary,
   finely chopped or ½
   teaspoon dried rosemary

1 tablespoon fresh basil, finely
   chopped or ½ teaspoon
   dried basil
the juice of half a lemon
5fl oz/150ml dry white wine,
   cider or apple juice
salt and freshly ground black
   pepper

1   Joint the rabbit into five pieces: two hind legs, the back cut into two and the front legs and ribcage as one piece. Sprinkle the paprika over the five rabbit pieces and brown them in the olive oil in a flameproof casserole.

2   Remove and set aside the rabbit pieces and brown the celery, leek and carrot. Take the pan off the heat and stir in the bay leaves, rosemary, basil. Season with salt and pepper.

3   Place the rabbit pieces on the vegetables in the casserole. Quickly heat up the lemon juice and wine, cider or apple juice and pour this over the rabbit and vegetables. Cover the pot (if the lid is not a tight fit, cover with a layer of foil as well) and place in the oven at 350°F/180°C/gas mark 4 for 1½ hours. Check after an hour and add a little water if necessary.

Slow Roast Chicken

If you are lucky enough to be able to buy a chicken that has actually been running about a farmyard, then this will be a good way of cooking it. Any chicken, free-range or not, will be cooked well by this method, but the flavour of a free-range bird will be far superior.

SERVES 4

1 3lb/1.4kg chicken, with
  giblets
2 tablespoons butter
a bunch of parsley
1 tablespoon olive oil
1 large carrot, finely chopped
1 medium onion, finely
  chopped

1 teaspoon dried thyme
2 tablespoons dry cider or
  white wine
salt and freshly ground black
  pepper

1   Put the giblets on one side and place the butter and parsley inside the chicken. Brush the bird all over with the olive oil, and sprinkle a little salt and pepper onto the breast.

2   Place the chopped carrot, onion and dried thyme in an oven-proof casserole and lay the chicken on top. Rinse the giblets under the cold tap and place them around the chicken, add the dry cider or white wine and enough water to come an inch up the side of the bird.

3   Cover the casserole and place in the oven at 300°F/150°C/gas mark 2 for 2½–3 hours, or even longer if the bird is an old one. Baste the chicken with the juices twice during the cooking time. When the chicken is cooked and nicely browned remove it and carve. Strain the contents of the pan and reduce the liquid quickly for a well flavoured gravy.

Chicken Salad

If you have leftover chicken from another meal use it for this delicious salad. Or buy a small chicken just for the purpose!

SERVES 4

1 cooked chicken (either poached or roasted as on page 144) or 1½–2lb/700–900g cooked meat

6 tomatoes, each cut into eight

3 sticks of celery, sliced

2 Cox's apples, cored and chopped

1 Cos lettuce

a bunch of parsley, finely chopped

freshly ground black pepper

Dressing

2 tablespoons yoghurt

1 tablespoon mayonnaise

2 tablespoons olive oil or 1 tablespoon olive oil and 1 tablespoon walnut oil

2 teaspoons red wine or cider vinegar

1 teaspoon tomato purée

1 teaspoon paprika

2 tablespoons finely chopped walnuts

1   Cut the cold chicken into cubes, discarding any bone or gristle. Mix together in a bowl with the tomatoes, celery and apple.

2   Make the dressing by mixing together all the ingredients and then add to the chicken mixture.

3   Lay the lettuce leaves on a large shallow bowl or dish, and spoon the salad carefully into the leaves. Just before serving, sprinkle the parsley and a little black pepper over the salad.

Chicken Curry

The parsnips are an unusual ingredient in this curry, but they add a sweetness which combines well with the aromatic curry powder. If you are using an older chicken it will probably need longer in the oven.

SERVES 4

1 3lb/1.4kg chicken
3 tablespoons olive oil
1 large onion, finely chopped
4 cloves garlic, finely chopped
4 tablespoons Kashmiri curry powder or other aromatic medium curry powder
4oz/110g button mushrooms, left whole

1 medium parsnip, thinly sliced
1lb/450g fresh tomatoes, roughly chopped, plus 2 tablespoons tomato purée or 1 14oz/400g tin of tomatoes
5–10fl oz/150–275ml water

1 Joint the chicken into four and cut each joint into three roughly even-sized pieces.

2 In a flameproof casserole heat the olive oil and soften the onion and garlic over a medium heat. Stir in the curry powder. Add the twelve chicken pieces and fry, turning several times, for 5–8 minutes, until lightly browned.

3 Add the mushrooms and parsnip and cook for a further 5 minutes, stirring now and again. Add the tomatoes (and purée if you are using it), and the water.

4 Cover and cook in the oven at 350°F/180°C/gas mark 4 for about 1 hour, or longer if you are using an older chicken (check after an hour to see if the curry needs a little more water).

Chicken Sauté

SERVES 4

1 3lb/1.4kg chicken *or* 4
   chicken joints (leg or
   breast)
3 tablespoons sunflower oil
1lb/450g small new potatoes,
   scrubbed
5 cloves garlic, skinned but left
   whole

1 wine glass of white wine or
   dry cider
1 teaspoon shoyu
1 bunch of spring onions,
   chopped
3 tablespoons finely chopped
   fresh parsley

1   If you have a whole chicken joint it into four. Cut each joint into three pieces of roughly the same size. Heat 2 tablespoons of the sunflower oil in a deep flameproof casserole and sauté the twelve chicken pieces for 10 minutes, turning several times. Remove the chicken pieces and set aside.

2   Add the potatoes and garlic cloves to the pan and sauté for 10 minutes, adding the rest of the sunflower oil if needed.

3   Take the pan off the heat, put back the chicken pieces and add the wine or cider and the shoyu to the potatoes. Cover the casserole and place in the oven at 375°F/190°C/gas mark 5 for 30–40 minutes, until the chicken is well cooked. Add the spring onions and parsley to the chicken a few minutes before the end.

Italian Lamb and Chestnuts

Do buy organically reared lamb if you can find it. Rare-breed lamb and mutton tends to have a better flavour and texture than 'ordinary' varieties, partly because of the breeds but also because it has probably not been raised under intensive conditions.

This lamb is excellent eaten with a sharp green salad, including rocket, chicory, radicchio or dandelion if possible.

SERVES 4

leg of lamb, weighing approximately 4lb/1.8kg, boned (ask your butcher to do this for you, and keep the bone)

2 or 3 sprigs of fresh rosemary *or* 2 teaspoons dried rosemary

3 cloves garlic, thinly sliced

2 tablespoons hazelnut or walnut oil

1 tablespoon olive oil

2 large onions, one chopped and one sliced into thin rings

4oz/110g dried chestnuts

2 tablespoons tomato purée

1¼ pints/700ml water

salt and freshly ground black pepper

1　Season the lamb with a little salt and pepper, and push two or three rosemary sprigs or the dried rosemary into the cavity left by the bone. Make a few small cuts in the lamb and insert slices of garlic. Tie the lamb tightly into a roll. Brown the lamb in the hazelnut or walnut oil in a large flameproof casserole on top of the stove. After browning, cover the pot and place in a medium oven, 350°F/180°C/gas mark 4, for one hour.

2　Meanwhile, heat the olive oil in a pan and brown the chopped onion. Add the lamb bone, dried chestnuts, tomato purée and water, cover and simmer for 45 minutes to 1 hour until the chestnuts are just soft. Discard the bone and strain the stock into a clean pan, setting aside the cooked chestnuts. Reduce the stock over a medium heat for 10 minutes.

3　Place the chestnuts around the lamb and pour on the reduced stock. Cover the lamb with the thinly sliced onion rings and return the uncovered casserole to the oven for a further 30–45 minutes, until the lamb is cooked.

4   Carve the lamb and arrange on a dish, surrounded with the chestnuts and onions. To make a strong sauce the stock can be reduced further, keeping it very hot to pour onto the lamb as it is served.

Autumn Lamb

This flavoursome dish is a real reward after a long day outside. Baked potatoes, cooked in the oven at the same time as the stew, and lightly cooked sprouts (see page 82) make this into a delicious meal.

SERVES 4

2lb/900g boned shoulder of
   lamb
3 tablespoons flour
2 tablespoons olive oil
1 teaspoon cinnamon
2 medium onions, finely
   chopped
2 cloves garlic, finely chopped
1 tablespoon dried mint

4 Cox's apples, peeled, cored
   and chopped
10fl oz/275ml dry cider
15fl oz/400ml water
4 tablespoons fresh mint, well
   washed and finely chopped
salt and freshly ground black
   pepper

1   Cut the meat into 1in/2.5cm cubes. Season the flour with salt and pepper and coat the meat cubes with it.

2   Brown the seasoned meat in the oil for 5–8 minutes in a heavy flameproof casserole.

3   Add the cinnamon, onion, garlic, dried mint and apple and brown carefully for a further 3–5 minutes.

4   Pour on the cider and water and bring to the boil. Turn down the heat, cover and simmer on the top of the stove or in the oven at 375°F/190°C/gas mark 5 for about 1½ hours or until the meat is tender. Stir in the fresh mint after 1 hour.

Stuffed Breast of Lamb

Breast is the cheapest cut of lamb to buy, it has a good flavour and is a versatile meat to cook. If you have the chance to buy the lean meat from some rare or primitive breeds do so, as it will probably have been reared extensively by a careful small scale producer. Ask your local butcher.

SERVES 4

> 1 breast of lamb, boned (ask your butcher to do this for you)
> 2 tablespoons olive oil

Stuffing

> 1 medium onion, chopped to a pulp
> 3 cloves garlic, finely chopped
> juice and grated peel of half a lemon
> ½ teaspoon freshly ground coriander
> 6oz/175g wholemeal breadcrumbs
> ½ teaspoon dried marjoram
> ½ teaspoon dried thyme
> 1 egg
> 2fl oz/50ml water
> 5 black olives, stoned and chopped, optional
> 8 walnut halves, finely chopped, optional
> salt and freshly ground black pepper

1   Mix together all the stuffing ingredients, adding the olives and walnuts if you are using them.

2   Remove any excess fat from the breast with a sharp knife. Lay the breast, fat side down, on a large plate and spread the stuffing evenly over the whole surface of the flesh. Roll up the meat, starting at the wide end (the narrow end will wrap round rather like a tail). Secure the roll with a couple of skewers, and brush with the olive oil. Place on a wire rack in a roasting tin and roast in the oven at 375°F/190°C/gas mark 5 for about 1 hour, until the meat is cooked;

the time needed will vary slightly, depending on the weight of your breast of lamb. Turn the meat over after 45 minutes.

3   Remove from the oven and carve into fine slices, using a sharp carving knife. Served either hot or cold.

Mutton Hot-pot

Mutton is the meat traditionally used for a hot-pot. Though it is now rather difficult to buy, its flavour is superior to that of lamb so do try it if you have the chance. Mutton needs a longer cooking time than lamb, and so if you are unable to find mutton and have to use lamb, cook it for 3 hours in the oven instead of the 4 hours recommended here.

SERVES 4

1½lb/700g mutton scrag end or stewing lamb, roughly diced
3 medium carrots, thickly sliced
4 medium onions, thinly sliced
1½lb/700g potatoes, thinly sliced

1 teaspoon dried rosemary
1 teaspoon dried thyme
1 tablespoon olive oil
salt and freshly ground black pepper

1   Arrange alternate layers of the vegetables and the meat in an ovenproof casserole, sprinkling each layer with a pinch or two of black pepper, salt and herbs and finishing with a layer of potato slices. Pour in enough water to come halfway up the casserole and brush the top with the olive oil.

2   Cover and place in the oven at 400°F/200°C/gas mark 6 for 30 minutes. Reduce the temperature to 275°F/140°C/gas mark 1 and continue to cook for 3 hours (2 hours if you are using lamb) more. Remove the lid for the last 30 minutes or so, to brown the potatoes.

Shepherd's Pie

Badly cooked Shepherd's Pie can be an example of the worst kind of 'institutional' food. However, if cooked carefully and with a little imagination it is a classic, enjoyable dish. Many people use minced beef, but traditionally it is cooked using lamb's tails; this recipe keeps to the same creature but uses the more readily available boned shoulder. If you buy ready-minced lamb check that it is lean – some butchers use breast of lamb for their mince, which is too fatty and also rather more expensive than shoulder of lamb.

SERVES 4

1¼lb/550g boned shoulder of lamb, minced *or* minced lamb from the butcher
2 tablespoons olive oil
2 medium onions, sliced into fine rings
1 medium carrot, finely chopped
2 cloves garlic, finely chopped

1 tablespoon tomato purée
1 teaspoon dried thyme
10–15fl oz/275–400ml water
1½lb/700g potatoes, peeled
2oz/50g butter
5fl oz/150ml milk
salt and freshly ground black pepper

1   Heat the oil in a heavy flameproof pot or casserole and cook the onion, carrot and garlic until soft. Add the minced lamb and over a fairly high heat stir the mixture rapidly, to seal and brown as much of the meat as possible. Add the tomato purée, the dried thyme and a little salt and pepper. Pour in the water, cover and simmer for 10–15 minutes.

2   Meanwhile, boil the potatoes, drain and mash with the butter and milk, and season with salt and pepper.

3   Take the lamb off the heat and fork the mashed potato carefully over the top. Place the pot without the lid in the oven at 350°F/180°C/gas mark 4 to bake for about 1 hour, until golden and crispy.

PUDDINGS AND CAKES

Many cooks reserve puddings for special meals, offering simply fresh fruit on an everyday basis. Some of these puddings are very light, others are warming and more substantial. All, however, are based on fresh fruit and use just enough sugar to ensure a sweet result. Several are very quick to prepare or energy-efficient to cook.

Toffee Apple Pudding

A good idea for using the winter abundance of Bramley apples. Don't add any sugar to the apple base of the pudding – save it all for the topping. If you allow the pudding to cool a little before serving the topping becomes quite crisp and almost like caramel.

SERVES 4

2lb/900g cooking apples, peeled, cored and chopped	2½oz/60g light muscovado sugar
4oz/110g margarine	2oz/50g fine wholemeal flour

1   Stew the apples in a little water to form a smooth purée. Transfer to an ovenproof dish and allow to cool.

2   Cream the margarine with the sugar until light and fluffy. Stir in the flour, mixing well. Carefully spread as evenly as possible over the cooled apple.

3   Bake in the oven at 400°F/200°C/gas mark 6 for 15–20 minutes. Alternatively, cook under a low–medium grill for about 10 minutes, taking care not to scorch the topping. For the best results you will need to use a dish that is not too high under the grill. Cool a little before serving.

Clementine Pudding

Serve this pudding warm with thick cream, fromage frais or Greek-style yoghurt. Clementines are used here, but experiment with other fruits – greengages or plums would be excellent.

SERVES 4–6

4oz/110g margarine
2oz/50g light muscovado sugar
1 large egg, beaten
2 tablespoons milk
6oz/175g fine wholemeal flour

1 teaspoon baking powder
4 clementines, peeled and
  divided into segments
1 teaspoon ground cinnamon
1 tablespoon clear honey

1   Cream the margarine with the sugar until light and fluffy. Carefully add the egg and the milk. Sift in the flour and baking powder and mix well.

2   Grease an 8in/20.5cm shallow baking dish. Put the clementines in the dish, sprinkle with the cinnamon and pour over the honey. Cover with the flour and egg mixture. Bake in a moderate oven, 350°F/180°C/gas mark 4, for 35–40 minutes until the top is cooked through.

Plum Crème Brûlée

This simple variation of the traditional pudding is far easier and quicker to make. Use very ripe plums or any other soft summer fruit – try strawberries or raspberries moistened with a little apple juice, or try some lightly cooked cherries or blackberries. I have used Greek-style yoghurt, as its good creamy flavour is ideal, but you could use fromage frais or whipped double cream instead.

SERVES 4

6 large, juicy plums	4 tablespoons brown sugar
½ pint/275ml Greek-style yoghurt	3 tablespoons water

1   Peel the plums if the skins are thick, then halve and stone them and divide between four individual serving dishes.

2   Divide the yoghurt between the four dishes, spooning evenly over the top of the plums.

3   Put the sugar into a small, heavy pan, add the water and bring to the boil over a moderate heat, stirring to dissolve the sugar. Boil for several minutes until the sugar starts to darken and caramelise. Remove from the heat and pour a little onto the yoghurt in each dish. Chill for 20–30 minutes before serving.

Fruit Soup

Wonderful on a hot summer's day, this chilled 'soup' uses buttermilk, the liquid left after the churning of cream into butter.

SERVES 4

2 ripe peaches
8oz/225g ripe strawberries
1 pint/570ml buttermilk

1   Peel the peaches, remove the stones and chop very finely. Mash the strawberries and add to the peaches with all the juice.

2   Add the buttermilk to the fruit purée and mix together gently. Chill before serving or add crushed ice and serve immediately.

Apricot Fool

A no-cook pudding that is rich and luxurious. For a more every-day effect use Greek-style yoghurt instead of double cream. Hunza apricots can be bought from wholefood shops – they are beautifully sweet, untreated and sundried wild apricots, resembling large nutmegs. To make a classic summer fool, use puréed soft fruits, such as strawberries or raspberries, instead of the apricots. Add sugar as desired and omit the flaked almonds.

SERVES 4

8oz/225g hunza apricots
½ pint/275ml double cream
1oz/25g flaked almonds

1   Soak the apricots overnight in cold water, or cover with boiling water and leave for several hours. Drain, remove the stones and chop the fruit as finely as possible.

2   Whip the cream until it forms soft peaks. Gently stir in the fruit and divide between four individual serving dishes. Set to cool in the fridge for 2–3 hours, or if you prefer you could put the fool in a large dish in the freezer for 2 hours, stirring once or twice during this time, to produce a semi-frozen effect. Sprinkle with the flaked almonds before serving.

Stir-fried Fruit

Fruit salad in its many forms is a popular and obviously 'green' pudding, using fresh, unprocessed ingredients and very little energy. Stir-frying the fruit is an unusual way of serving a fruit salad, and brings out different flavours in the fruit. Here is a simple three-fruit combination based on home-grown ingredients.

SERVES 4

1 tablespoon sunflower oil	1oz/25g walnuts, chopped
2 ripe pears, finely sliced	2 tablespoons clear honey
2 eating apples, finely sliced	
4 ripe plums, stoned and halved	

1   Heat the oil in a large, heavy pan, add the pears and apples and cook over a medium heat for 2–3 minutes.

2   Add the plums and the walnuts, and continue to cook for 2–3 minutes, stirring constantly.

3   Stir in the honey over the heat and serve.

Fruit Fritters

SERVES 4

3oz/75g gram flour	4fl oz/100ml water
pieces of fruit – banana, apple, pear, plum, orange, etc.	2 tablespoons clear honey
	sunflower oil for frying

1   Put the flour into a bowl and gradually incorporate the water, mixing well to make a smooth batter

2   Heat enough oil to come a third of the way up a deep-sided frying-pan. Test with a little batter – if it sizzles, proceed with the fritters by dipping the pieces of fruit in the batter and dropping carefully into the hot oil. Fry quite quickly, turning during the cooking to brown the pieces evenly. Drain and serve immediately with a little honey drizzled over the top.

Note   If you prefer, you can grate apples or pears coarsely and add tiny pieces of banana or other fruits, to form a sweet 'bhajii'. Add the fruit mixture to the batter and then drop spoonfuls into the hot fat and cook as above.

Raspberry and Hazelnut Pavlova

Pavlova is quite simple to make, and special enough for any dinner party. This version is lower in sugar than the traditional pavlova, and though I have used double cream, Greek yoghurt and fromage frais are also good. Any soft fruit can be used – strawberries are also particularly successful. Use the leftover egg yolks to make mayonnaise, real custard or to thicken a soup.

SERVES 4–6

4oz/110g hazelnuts
4 egg whites
4oz/110g fine brown sugar

½ teaspoon vinegar
½ pint/275ml double cream
8oz/225g raspberries

1   Grease and flour two 8in/20.5cm sandwich tins. Set the oven at 325°F/170°C/gas mark 3. As the oven is heating up put the hazelnuts onto a baking tray and place at the top of the oven to brown. Remove from the oven after a few minutes and rub off the loose skins. Chop the nuts finely using a large cook's knife or a grinder.

2   Whisk the egg whites until stiff. Using a metal spoon carefully fold in the sugar, a little at a time, and the vinegar, and then add the chopped nuts in the same way. Divide the mixture between the two tins and bake in the middle of the oven for about 30 minutes, until the meringues are set and light brown. Remove from the oven, leave for a minute in the tins, and then turn out to cool on a wire rack. The meringues will be moist and sticky.

3   Whip the cream and pile two-thirds of it onto one of the meringues. Top with most of the raspberries and then gently place the second meringue on top. Spread with the remaining cream and chill for at least 1 hour. Decorate with the last few raspberries and serve.

Tarte Tatin

An upside-down apple pie – a great favourite from France and another way of using apples, surely the most successful British fruit. You may find this easier to make than the traditional English apple pie – especially if pastry-making is not your strong point – as in this recipe when the tart is turned out of the tin the pastry is completely covered by the apples.

SERVES 6 – 8

Pastry

8oz/225g unbleached plain white flour	5oz/150g unsalted butter
pinch of salt	1 egg, beaten
	cold water

Filling

3lb/1.4kg cooking apples, peeled and sliced	3oz/75g unsalted butter
	4oz/110g light brown sugar

1   To make the pastry, put the flour and salt into a bowl and rub in the butter until the mixture resembles fine breadcrumbs. Add the beaten egg and draw together, adding enough cold water to make a soft dough. Cover and leave to rest for 20–30 minutes in the fridge.

2   Grease a 10in/25cm diameter shallow baking dish (a glass one would be ideal) with a little butter.

3   To make the filling, melt the butter in a large pan, add the apples and sugar and cook over a high heat for about 5 minutes. Remove from the heat and pile the apples into the baking dish.

4   Roll out the pastry a little larger than the dish and cover the apples, pressing down the dough around the edges. Make one or two holes in the top to allow the steam to escape.

5   Bake in the oven at 400°F/200°C/gas mark 6 for 30–40 minutes, until the pastry is brown. Cool slightly and turn out onto a serving dish. Serve warm, with cream or yoghurt.

Luncheon Cake

This cut-and-come-again fruit cake is free from added sugar. It is lovely and moist and can be used for packed lunches, birthday cakes, or just as a cake for tea.

3oz/75g dates, chopped	1 teaspoon baking powder
3fl oz/75ml water	1 teaspoon cinnamon
4oz/110g vegetable margarine	4oz/110g raisins
2 eggs, beaten	2oz/50g currants
6oz/175g wholemeal flour	2 tablespoons orange juice

1   Put the dates into a small pan with the water, and simmer gently for 10 minutes, taking care that they don't burn. Remove from the heat, beat with a wooden spoon until smooth, and leave to cool.

2   When the dates are cool, cream them with the margarine until light. Stir in the eggs one at a time with a little flour, mixing well. Sieve the rest of the flour with the baking powder and the cinnamon, and gently fold into the cake mixture. Add the raisins, currants and orange juice, adding a little extra juice if necessary to make a dropping consistency.

3   Spoon the mixture into a lightly greased 2lb/900g loaf tin, and bake in a moderate oven, 350°F/180°C/gas mark 4 for 40–45 minutes, until risen and firm to the touch. Allow to cool in the tin for 5 minutes, and turn out onto a cooling rack.

Yankee Carrot Cake

You can eat this cake just as it is, or with the simple topping described below.

4fl oz/100ml sunflower oil
3oz/75g muscovado sugar
2 eggs
6oz/175g fine wholemeal flour
1 teaspoon baking powder
1 teaspoon ground cinnamon

6oz/175g carrots, finely grated
2oz/50g walnuts, roughly
  chopped
grated rind and juice of 1
  lemon

Topping

4oz/110g cream cheese
1oz/25g caster sugar
grated rind of 1 orange

1   Put the oil, sugar and eggs into a large bowl and whisk together until the mixture is smooth and thick.

2   Sieve the flour, baking powder and cinnamon into the egg mixture and mix in gently, using a metal spoon. Add the carrots, walnuts and the lemon rind and juice, again mixing well.

3   Spoon the mixture into a greased 8in/20.5cm cake tin, and bake in a moderate oven, 375°F/190°C/gas mark 5, for 25–30 minutes, until the cake is risen and firm. Turn out and cool on a wire rack.

4   Mix together the topping ingredients and spread over the cooled cake.

INTERESTING EXTRAS

Herb and Fruit Vinegars

Making herb and fruit vinegars is a lovely way to extend the enjoyment of your home-grown herbs, and to savour the flavours of herbs or fruits out of season. The vinegars are mildly flavoured and pleasantly aromatic. Here are just two of many possibilities.

Raspberry Vinegar

Add 3oz/75g fresh raspberries to 1 pint/570ml organic cider vinegar. Seal the jar, leave to stand for 2–3 weeks, and then strain. Use as vinegar in salad dressings and add to sweet and sour sauces and to stir-fries.

Basil and Garlic Vinegar

Add 3 whole cloves of garlic and a few sprigs of fresh basil to 1 pint/570ml white wine vinegar. Leave for 2 weeks and then strain and use as above.

Note When choosing herbs to add to vinegar pick the leaves before the plant has flowered. After straining the vinegar you can add a sprig of fresh herb for extra flavour – it also looks most attractive in the bottle.

Dried Apple Rings

If you have your own apple tree, or an endless supply of apples from some other source, drying the apples is a good method of preserving them for use all year round.

Peel and core the apples using a stainless steel knife. Slice into rings about ¼in/0.5cm thick. Plunge immediately into water with lemon juice added and leave for 10 minutes. Drain and thread the rings onto strings and hang in a warm place like an airing cupboard for several hours until the apples are dry but still soft. Alternatively, you can dry the apples in a very cool oven. Cool the dried apple rings and then pack into a dry jar or tin. To cook the dried apple rings, soak overnight in water and then cook in the soaking liquid.

Olive Paste

It is useful to know how to make olive paste as it is so versatile; you can use it as a simple first course spread on circles of toast and garnished with red pepper and lemon, as a more robust sandwich filling with tomatoes and lettuce, or as a basis for an exciting pasta dish (see page 106). Buy your olives loose from delicatessens or choose the Greek black olives in jars. They are preserved in salt and are particularly moist without being too sharp.

MAKES A SMALL POT

4oz/110g black olives, stoned
1–2 tablespoons lemon juice
3–4 tablespoons olive oil *or*
   2oz/50g butter

2–3 tablespoons fresh
   breadcrumbs (optional)

1   Chop the olives very finely with a cook's knife until they are almost puréed. If you have a mincer you can pass the olives through this.

2   Mix the olives with the lemon juice and the olive oil or butter. If you are using butter it will help if you first soften the butter in a bowl with a wooden spoon. If you would like the paste to be quite solid then mix in the breadcrumbs. Chill before serving.

Yoghurt

Many of the recipes in this book use yoghurt – it is very easy and economical to make your own yoghurt at home. It is worth using a thermometer to make sure the milk is at the right temperature.

MAKES 1 PINT/570ML

> 1 pint/570ml milk
> 1 tablespoon live yoghurt from
>   a bought pot

1   Warm a wide-necked, perfectly clean vacuum flask by rinsing with boiling water.

2   Bring the milk to the boil, remove from the heat and allow to cool to 45°C. Pour the cooled milk into the warmed flask and add the yoghurt, stirring to mix well. Put the stopper in the flask and leave for 6–7 hours. Turn the yoghurt out of the flask and store in a fridge.

Greek-style Yoghurt

To turn your home-made yoghurt into Greek-style yoghurt, simply put the yoghurt into a nylon sieve and allow it to drip over a bowl for 1–2 hours. The thick, creamy mild yoghurt left in the sieve will be as good as any Greek-style yoghurt that you might buy.

INDEX